D0931208

THE PLACE OF WESLEY
IN THE
CHRISTIAN TRADITION

*Essays delivered at Drew University
in celebration of the commencement of
the publication of the Oxford Edition
of the Works of John Wesley*

edited by
KENNETH E. ROWE

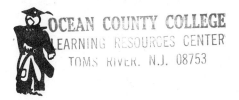
The Scarecrow Press, Inc.
Metuchen, N.J.   1976

Library of Congress Cataloging in Publication Data
Main entry under title:

The Place of Wesley in the Christian tradition.

   "Essays delivered at Drew University in celebration
of the commencement of the publication of the Oxford
edition of the works of John Wesley."
   Bibliography: p.
   Includes index.
   1. Wesley, John, 1703-1791—Addresses, essays,
lectures. I. Rowe, Kenneth A.
BX8495.W5P53   287'.092'4   76-27659
ISBN 0-8108-0981-8

CONTENTS

EDITOR'S INTRODUCTION

THE SEARCH FOR THE HISTORICAL WESLEY

Wesley's Place in the Christian tradition has always
been difficult to determine.   Friend and foe alike through
successive generations have sought to document his theological pedigree.   Contemporary and polemical interests through
the years have often clouded rather than clarified these efforts.   Much too has depended on whether the focus was on
Wesley's doctrinal theology or his practical churchmanship.
While a full-scale critical assessment of the literature still
remains to be done, this volume marks a substantial beginning.

Early 19th-century Methodists on both sides of the Atlantic, anxious to suppress Wesley's "catholic connection" to
the Church of England, celebrated instead his "Protestant"
conversion from all things catholic at Aldersgate.   Thomas
Jackson's omission of Wesley's extract of the Homilies of the
Church of England attributed to Cranmer in what until now has
been the "standard" edition of his works (14 volumes, London,
1829-31) is a good example.   Despite the fact that Wesley
claimed the Homilies as authoritative, published no fewer than
twenty editions in his lifetime, and included the extract in the
collected works which he himself published in 1771-1774,
Jackson chose to bury it. [1]

A generation later the emergence of the Oxford Move-

ment in England and the "high church" party among American
Episcopalians sparked interest in Wesley's catholic churchmanship.   Methodist evangelicals, however, preferred to ignore charges that they were unfaithful heirs of Wesley in
thought and practice.   Main stream British Methodism's lin-
gering dream of being adopted by mother church was shattered and she became more self-consciously Noncomformist.
American Methodists became militantly "low church," prefer-
ring to ignore Wesley's concern for liturgy and sacraments,
and staunchly revivalist, reducing his concern for the full
range of theological problems to a theology of conversion.
Echoes of Wesley's catholic past were heard in the 1880s,
but the project of Methodist theologians William B. Pope in
England and Thomas O. Summers in America to recover
classical Wesleyanism proved to be a mere "Indian summer
of orthodoxy."[2]   Through the end of the century the pietist
portrait of Wesley as the warm-hearted evangelist went largely unchallenged.   Victorian Nonconformity in England and
evangelical revivalism in America severely narrowed the
horizon of Methodism's original focus and profoundly shaped
a century of Wesley biographers, editors, and interpreters.

Methodism underwent a major theological shift at the
end of the century.   "Liberal" Protestantism, which had been
developing in Europe since Schleiermacher in the 1820s,
caught up with the Methodists in the 1890s.   The new theological fashion called for no major overhaul of Wesley--a
simple updating from Wesley the evangelist to Wesley the
theologian of experience would do.[3]   Methodism's conversion
to liberalism coincided with the climax of a long quarrel with
a restless holiness movement within.   Following their own
version of Wesley on Christian Perfection and the spirit-filled
life, the Holiness folk "went out" to form independent holiness

churches in his name.

George Croft Cell's rediscovery that Wesley was "orthodox" in 1935 marked the beginning of a new search for the historical Wesley. The revival of Reformation studies sponsored by "Neo-Orthodoxy" led some scholars to trace Wesley's lineage back to the Continental Reformers--Cell to Calvin and Franz Hildebrandt to Luther, for example. [4] Other scholars like Martin Schmidt and Clifford W. Towlson detected and documented Wesley's links to Continental Pietism and Moravianism in particular;[5] Jean Orcibal to the Western mystical tradition;[6] Maximin Piette and John Todd to Roman Catholicism;[7] Horton Davies, Robert Monk and John Newton to English Puritanism. [8] John Deschner found Wesley to be "proto-Barthian. "[9] Albert Outler described him as a virtual Ante-Nicene Father REDIVIVUS. [10] Arthur M. Allchin and Marcus Ward saw affinities with Eastern Orthodoxy. [11] Leo Cox, Claude Thompson, George Turner, Mildred Wynkoop and others claimed Wesley for the Holiness tradition. [12] Ole Borgen, Garth Lean, Lawrence McIntosh, J. Ernest Rattenbury, Gordon Rupp, Paul Sanders and Albert Outler revived the label Wesley himself preferred--"Anglican in Earnest. "[13]

H. Richard Niebuhr and, more recently, James Gustafson have dusted off Wesley as a resource for Christian ethics. [14] The Ecumenical Movement and Vatican II have inspired others to see Wesley as a significant ecumenical theologian--John Deschner, Colin Williams, and Michael Hurley. [15] Pentocostalists like David J. DuPlessis and Charismatics like Robert G. Tuttle have "discovered" Wesley as a model for their spirit-filled movements. [16] Although more interested in effect than cause, recent historians such as Bernard Semmel, Edward P. Thompson and W. Reginald Ward see Wesley as a social revolutionary. [17] And of course a host of folk--inside and

outside the Methodist camp--continue to cling to the traditional
portrait of Wesley as the "Patron Saint of Theological Indiffer-
entism. "

    Part of the blame for the unbelievably wide range of
labels which have been applied to Wesley then and now may be
due to the fact that he was destined to be interpreted through
woefully incomplete, poorly edited, and largely unannotated
sources.   Unlike Luther or Calvin scholars, Augustine or
Aquinas researchers, students of Wesley have never had a
complete and scholarly edition of his writings.   Wesley himself issued a

> 'collected edition' in his own lifetime (32 volumes
> printed by William Pine in Bristol in 1771-74)
> [which] was naturally incomplete and sadly marred
> by careless printing.   The second edition, with
> Joseph Benson as editor (17 volumes printed in Lon-
> don, 1809-13), was more complete but no more
> critical.   The Benson edition was then republished
> in Philadelphia and New York (10 volumes) in 1826-
> 27, and advertised as the 'First American Edition. '
> A 'third edition' was published by Thomas Jackson
> (14 volumes, London, 1829-31), and this has re-
> mained ever since as the basic edition of Wesley's
> 'collected works. '   It has often been reprinted but
> never revised; its lack of a critical apparatus never
> repaired.   A photo-offset reproduction of the 1872
> reprint of the Jackson edition was recently published
> (1958-59), and advertised as 'the first complete un-
> abridged edition in early 100 years!'   Modern edi-
> tions of The Journal (Nehemiah Curnock, ed.), the
> so-called Standard Sermons (E. H. Sugden, ed.) and
> Letters (John Telford, ed.) represent major ad-
> vances over the 'Jackson' edition.   However, they
> comprise only a small fraction of Wesley's author-
> ship and, even so, are far from adequate. [18]

In the meantime a breakthrough has occurred in deciphering
the shorthand of Wesley's Oxford diaries, enough new letters
have surfaced to fill at least another large volume, and a
large batch (100 plus) of "unstandard" sermons has been

largely overlooked and unprinted. In short, one of Christendom's most prolific authors and editors has been badly represented on library shelves. No wonder, as Professor Outler
once remarked, Wesley has been more revered than read,
more eulogized than understood.

A dozen years ago Wesley scholars from four American Methodist seminaries--Robert E. Cushman of Duke, Franz
Hildebrandt of Drew, John Lawson of Candler at Emory and
Albert C. Outler of Perkins--called for a new comprehensive
and critical edition of Wesley's principal writings in order to
document more adequately his contributions to both catholic
and evangelical Christianity. An editorial committee formulated plans, encouraged their universities to fund the project,
enlisted an international and ecumenical team of scholars as
editors, and persuaded the press of Wesley's venerable alma
mater to publish the product.

In the fall of 1974, Protestant and Catholic scholars
from England, Germany, Ireland, and the United States gath-
ered at Drew University in Madison, New Jersey to celebrate
the commencement of the publication of the Oxford Edition of
the works of John Wesley. Directly and indirectly, most of
them have played leading roles in the project: Professors
Frank Baker, Albert C. Outler, E. Gordon Rupp and Martin
Schmidt, along with Father Michael Hurley and Bishop James
K. Mathews, presented the principal addresses. Professors
Robert E. Cushman, Horton Davies, John T. Ford, Lawrence
D. McIntosh, F. Ernest Stoeffler, and J. Robert Wright,
along with Dean Colin Williams and Bishop James W. Malone,
participated as respondents. The Consultation was funded by
the Ezra Squier Tipple Lectureship of the Theological School
and the Arlo Ayres Brown Lectureship of the Graduate School
at Drew University.

Although planned two years earlier as a "Christening
party" for the Oxford edition, the affair turned out to be
merely a baby shower, for actual publication was delayed.
Proof copies, however, of the first of 33 volumes to appear,
which includes Wesley's "Appeals to Men of Reason and Religion" and certain related open letters edited by Gerald R.
Cragg (volume 11), were displayed.   Actual publication by
Oxford University Press did not take place until February of
1976.

The theme of the Drew Consultation was "The Place
of Wesley in the Christian Tradition."   Full texts of the five
principal addresses follow.   The papers bristle with insights
into Wesley sources.   Albert Outler calls attention to Wesley's typically Anglican interest in the early church fathers.
Gordon Rupp reinforces his unfaltering allegiance to the
Church of England.   Martin Schmidt traces again the formative influence of Continental Pietism on the young Wesley.

The major preoccupation of the Consultation papers,
however, is not Wesley's sources, but rather with Wesley
as a resource for contemporary theology and churchmanship.
Our authors are not so much interested in Wesley himself
but in what Wesley was interested in.   Though classical
church controversies are long dead, notes Outler,

> the concerns that were advanced and defended in those
> controversies are still with us. ...   There still is no
> assuagement from the pain and emptiness and hunger
> of the human heart for a meaningful life and a mean-
> ingful death.   And there can be none apart from God's
> grace gracefully received... or apart from "holy liv-
> ing" (God's grace enabling human love to flower and
> fruit in happiness, personal and communal).

It is Jesuit Michael Hurley who breaks new ground in his reflections on "Salvation Today and John Wesley Today" by showing the theological significance of Wesley's concept of pre-

venient grace, the universality of grace in creation, for current discussion of mission and evangelism and especially for
the contemporary interreligious dialogue.

Professor Baker describes the development of the Oxford edition project and the baffling problem of determining
definitive texts of Wesley's principal writings.   We have also
included Professor McIntosh's splendid Consultation bibliography on Wesley studies.

Our hope is that these essays, and the project they
celebrate, may stimulate fresh thought about Wesley's place
in the Christian tradition and about his significance for the
on-going theological task.

Kenneth E. Rowe

Drew University
Madison, New Jersey

NOTES

1 Lawrence D. McIntosh, "John Wesley: a problem in historiography," The Spectator (Melbourne) vol. XCIII,
   no. 8 (March 1, 1967), p. 4.   Albert C. Outler includes Wesley's extract plus judicious commentary in
   his John Wesley (New York: Oxford University Press,
   1964), pp. 121-133.

2 William B. Pope, A Compendium of Christian Theology,
   2d ed. , rev. & enl. (London: Wesleyan Conference
   Office, 1877-80), 3 vols.; Thomas O. Summers,
   Systematic Theology, a Complete Body of Wesleyan-
   Arminian Divinity Consisting of Lectures on the 25
   Articles of Religion (Nashville: Publishing House of
   the Methodist Episcopal Church, South, 1888), 2 vols.

3 For a later "Liberal" portrait of Wesley, see Umphrey
   Lee, John Wesley and Modern Religion (Nashville:
   Cokesbury Press, 1936).

4   George Croft Cell, The Rediscovery of John Wesley (New
    York: Henry Holt & Co., 1935); Franz Hildebrandt,
    From Luther to Wesley (London: Lutterworth Press,
    1951).

5   Martin Schmidt, John Wesley (Zurich: Gotthelf Verlag,
    1953-66), 2 vols.; English translation by Norman P.
    Goldhawk published under title John Wesley: A Theo-
    logical Biography (London: Epworth Press, 1962-73),
    3 vols. Clifford W. Towlson, Moravian and Methodist
    (London: Epworth Press, 1957).

6   Jean Orcibal, "Les spirituels français et espagnols chez
    John Wesley et ses contemporains," Révue de l'His-
    toire des Religions, vol. 139 (1951), pp. 50-109; "The
    Theological Originality of John Wesley and Continental
    Spirituality," in A History of the Methodist Church in
    Great Britain, edited by Rupert Davies and Gordon
    Rupp (London: Epworth Press, 1965), vol. I, pp. 83-
    111.

7   Maximin Piette, John Wesley in the Evolution of Protes-
    tantism (London: Sheed and Ward, 1937); John M.
    Todd, John Wesley and the Catholic Church (London:
    Hodder & Stoughton, 1958).

8   Horton Davies, Worship and Theology in England (Prince-
    ton, N.J.: Princeton University Press, 1961), vol. 3,
    chapter VII & VIII, pp. 143-209. Robert C. Monk,
    John Wesley, His Puritan Heritage (Nashville: Abing-
    don, 1966). John A. Newton, Methodism and the Puri-
    tans (London: Dr. Williams Library, 1964); Susanna
    Wesley and the Puritan Tradition in Methodism (Lon-
    don: Epworth Press, 1968).

9   John Deschner, Wesley's Christology, An Interpretation
    (Dallas: Southern Methodist University Press, 1960).
    A doctoral study at the University of Basel under Karl
    Barth.

10 Albert C. Outler, ed., John Wesley (New York: Oxford
    University Press, 1964) (Library of Protestant Thought).
    In another essay Outler adds the importance to Wesley
    of nominalism in late medieval catholicism: "Meth-
    odism's Theological Heritage: A Study in Perspective,"
    in Methodism's Destiny in an Ecumenical Age, edited
    by Paul M. Minus, Jr. (Nashville: Abingdon Press,

1969), pp. 44-70. See also his essay "John Wesley
as Theologian--then and now," Methodist History, vol.
12, no. 4 (July, 1974), pp. 63-82, and his Theology
in the Wesleyan Spirit (Nashville: Tidings, 1975).

11 Arthur M. Allchin, "Our Life in Christ: In John Wesley
and the Eastern Fathers" in We Belong to One Another,
Methodist, Anglican and Orthodox Essays, edited by
A. M. Allchin (London: Epworth Press, 1965), pp.
62-78; Marcus Ward, essay in Fellowship of St. Al-
bans & St. Sergius, The Dialogue of East and West in
Christendom (London: Faith Press, 1963), pp. 41-44.

12 Leo G. Cox, John Wesley's Concept of Perfection (Kansas
City, Mo.: Beacon Hill Press, 1964); Claude H.
Thompson, The Witness of American Methodism to the
Historical Doctrine of Christian Perfection, unpublished
Ph.D. thesis, Drew University, 1949; George A. Turn-
er, The More Excellent Way: The Scriptural Basis of
the Wesleyan Message (Winona Lake, Ind.: Light and
Life Press, 1952); Mildred B. Wynkoop, Foundations
of Wesleyan-Arminian Theology (Kansas City, Mo.:
Beacon Hill Press, 1967); A Theology of Love: The
Dynamic of Wesleyanism (Kansas City, Mo.: Beacon
Hill Press, 1972).

13 Ole E. Borgen, John Wesley on the Sacraments, A Theo-
logical Study (Nashville: Abingdon Press, 1972);
Garth Lean, John Wesley, Anglican (London: Bland-
ford, 1964); Lawrence D. McIntosh, The Nature and
Design of Christianity in John Wesley's Early Theology,
unpublished Ph.D. thesis, Drew University, 1966; John
E. Rattenbury, The Eucharistic Hymns of John and
Charles Wesley (London: Epworth Press, 1948); The
Conversion of the Wesleys (London: Epworth Press,
1938); E. Gordon Rupp, Methodism in Relation to the
Protestant Tradition (London: Epworth Press, 1951);
"Some Reflections on the origin and development of
the English Methodist tradition, 1738-1898," London
Quarterly & Holborn Review, vol. 178 (July, 1953);
pp. 166-175; Protestant Catholicity (London: Epworth
Press, 1960), and especially his essay in this volume;
Paul S. Sanders, "Wesley's Eucharistic Faith and
Practice," Anglican Theological Review, vol. 148, no.
2 (April, 1966), pp. 157-174; "The Puritans and John
Wesley," Work/Worship, vol. 17, no. 2 (Whitsuntide,
1967), pp. 13-19; "What God Hath Joined Together,"

Religion in Life, vol. 29, no. 4 (Autumn, 1960), pp.
491-500.

14   H. Richard Niebuhr, Christ and Culture (New York:
     Harper & Brothers, 1951), pp. 218f.; Kingdom of
     God in America (New York: Harper & Brothers,
     1937), passim; Christian Ethics, edited by Waldo
     Beach and H. Richard Niebuhr (New York: Ronald
     Press, 1955), chapter 12, pp. 353-379; James M.
     Gustafson, Christ and the Moral Life (New York:
     Harper & Row, 1968), chapter 3, pp. 61-83.

15   John Deschner, "The Role of Theology in the Church:
     One Holy, Catholic and Apostolic Church," in Proceed-
     ings of the World Methodist Conference, Denver, 1971,
     edited by Lee F. Tuttle (Nashville: Abingdon Press;
     London, Epworth Press, 1972), pp. 220-227; John A.
     Newton, "The Ecumenical Wesley," Ecumenical Review,
     vol. 24, no. 2 (April, 1972), pp. 160-175; John Wes-
     ley's Letter to a Roman Catholic, edited by Michael
     Hurley (Dublin: Geoffrey Chapman and Epworth House,
     1968); Colin Williams, John Wesley's Theology Today
     (Nashville: Abingdon Press, 1960).

16   David J. DuPlessis, The Spirit Bade Me Go; The As-
     tounding Move of God in the Denominational Churches
     (Plainfield, N.J.: Logos International, 1970). Robert
     G. Tuttle, "The Influence of Roman Catholic Mystics
     on John Wesley," unpublished doctoral dissertation,
     University of Bristol, England, 1970; The Partakers:
     Holy Spirit Power for the Persevering Christians
     (Nashville: Abingdon Press, 1974). Tuttle currently
     teaches at Fuller Theological Seminary in Pasadena,
     California.

17   Bernard Semmel, The Methodist Revolution (New York:
     Basic Books, Inc., 1973); Edward P. Thompson, The
     Making of the English Working Class (London: V.
     Gollancz, 1963); W. Reginald Ward, Religion and So-
     ciety in England 1790-1850 (London: Batsford, 1972).

18   Albert C. Outler, ed., John Wesley (New York: Oxford
     University Press, 1964), pp. ix-x.

CHAPTER I

THE PLACE OF WESLEY
IN THE CHRISTIAN TRADITION

Albert C. Outler

To write synoptically of John Wesley's "place" in the
Christian Tradition in a single essay is a bit intimidating.
A lifetime's study of the history of Christian thought has re-
sulted in no better than a smattering acquaintance with "the
Christian tradition," viewed as a historiographical problem.
A decade with Faith & Order's Theological Study Commission
on Tradition and Traditions (1952-1963) prompted a good deal
of pondering about this tradition, as a theological problem.
A dozen years spent with Wesley, now in my old age, has
opened up an exciting horizon of inquiry as to his place in
and import for the Christian tradition--now and tomorrow.
But, inevitably, the limits of this essay will force me to
broad generalizations without their full evidence and arguments.   To the offended or the skeptical, I can only plead
that there's a lot more where this came from.   The rest of
you, who prefer summaries to a full script, ought to be
thankful for what you are not about to receive!

Until our own times, certainly, Wesley's "place" was
clearly established (albeit with contrary evaluations): he was
the founder of Methodism.   For Methodist triumphalists this
was enough--one thinks of Tyerman's sincere paean: "Meth-

11

odism is the greatest fact in the history of the church."[1]
What this needed was an adequate etiology, and Wesley met
that need. To the radicals amongst Methodism's despisers
(e.g., E. P. Thompson) it was enough to fix on Wesley the
blame for Methodism's failures to support the revolutionary
aims of "the English working class."[2] Secular historians
(Halévy, Robertson, Semmel) have recognized Wesley's historical influence without probing deeply into the theological
basis for it (although Semmel is something of an exception
here--and his book is likely to stand as a landmark in Wesley studies for just this reason).[3]

Non-Methodists (with a few exceptions) have found
Wesley easy enough to ignore or else to assess in terms of
their own several traditions. Hildebrandt measured him by
the yardstick of Luther; Piette recognized the catholic elements in his doctrine but scarcely understood his Protestantism; Professor Schmidt has seen him as a crossbreed of
Puritanism and Pietism.[4] No major Calvinist historian (to
my knowledge) has studied him in depth--unless you reckon
Horton Davies as a "Calvinist"--but there have been Methodist scholars concerned to stress the "Puritan" elements in
Wesley's faith and thought (Cell, Newton, Monk). Anglicans,
generally, have been content to leave him to the Methodists.
Alexander Knox, Robert Southey (and Canon Overton) considered him an offbeat Anglican--and, in our time, there
have been specialized studies by men like Ronald Knox (quon-
dam Anglican), V. H. H. Green and Garth Lean. But none
of these regarded Wesley as a significant Anglican theologian
--and none attempted the unpacking of the huge jumble of his
sources as a way of explaining his resultant theological position. Roman Catholics, by and large (with a few happy exceptions like Fr. Hurley), have felt no need to go behind

Wesley's outspoken anti-Romanism to notice similarities and differences in his doctrines of justification as compared with the early debates on this subject at Trent (Seripando, Pole, Sanfelice)[5] or with Bellarmine in the later De Auxiliis controversy. No Roman whom I know has yet noticed (in print) the remarkable resonances between Wesley's teachings on "holiness of heart and life" and those remarkable chapters in Lumen Gentium, IV and V.

My own interest in Wesley has less to do with his stature and function as Methodism's cult-hero than with what I have come to regard as his significant achievements as a theologian--in his special historical situation. He has gone unnoticed by historical theologians, generally, partly because he was not a theologian's theologian, partly because he belonged to no single school and founded none. Wesley's lack of epigones needs further analysis, but not here and now. The historical theologian is bound to view mass evangelists and popularizers with suspicion, as being derivative or simplistic. "Landmark theologians" are more readily identified by their genius for, say, metaphysics (St. Augustine, St. Thomas) or hermeneutics (Luther) or system-building (Calvin). But Wesley was a folk-theologian--with no academic base (such as Luther had or the Halle pietists), no political base (Calvin and Knox) and no intention of founding a new denomination, even if one did emerge (over his dead body!).

On the other hand, we don't have many mass evangelists of record with anything like Wesley's immersion in classical culture, his eager openness to "modern" science and social change, his awareness of the entire Christian tradition as a living resource--and even fewer with his ecclesial vision of a sacramental community as the nurturing environment of Christian experience. One thinks of Richard Baxter,

Charles Simeon, St. John Bosco as possible analogs--each
comparable in some respects but not in all.

Thus a resultant thesis has been forming in my mind
in answer to this nagging puzzle--"How best to characterize
this man?"--that John Wesley was the most important Anglican theologian of the 18th century because of his distinctive,
composite answer to the age-old question as to "the nature of
the Christian life": its origins, growth, imperatives, social
impact, final end. Over five decades in a revival that he directed solo, less by foresight than shrewd reaction, his constant
problematic was soteriology--amongst people who had few in-
centives to be comforted by verbal or abstract answers.
Everything creative in his theologizing (including his sources
and his way with them) has this practical concern as its warrant. This explains his hermeneutics (sola Scriptura), his
appeals to tradition, his impulse to controversy, his tenuous
alliances with other evangelicals, his gallant "appeals to men
of reason and religion," etc.

This root question as to the nature of Christian existence had first been defined for him at Epworth--largely in
his theological tutorials with his mother (continued by correspondence from Oxford). It had been redefined in his am-
bivalent experiences in the Holy Club; it had been brought into focus in his confrontations with the Moravians and Salzburgers in Georgia; it had turned into an agonizing groping
for faith with Peter Böhler. The agony had been resolved
--dramatically and for a time--at Aldersgate, but the larger
problem continued to press upon him throughout the unfolding
drama of the Revival and his further theological reflections.
He denied that he ever changed his theological position after
1738, partly because his basic intentions had never changed.
But the nuances and equilibria of the position did change and

these changes are the only clues I have found to explain his
otherwise incredible eclecticism: e.g., that theological med-
ley in The Christian Library, those strange exhumations in
The Arminian Magazine.

Within the terms of this hypothesis, one can set the
succession of Wesley's theological stages in a credible perspective and, even more importantly, comprehend, at least
in part, the dynamics of the Wesleyan syndrom (repentance,
justification-regeneration-sanctification), the Wesleyan aversion
to antinomianism ("speculative" and "practical"), [6] the Wesleyan
doctrine of grace, the Wesleyan wedding of the evangelical
principle with the catholic substance of Christianity. In short,
it was Wesley's distinctive undertaking to integrate "faith
alone" with "holy living" in an authentic dialectic.

Everyone knows that the antithesis of "faith alone" and
"holy living" was the most tortured issue in classical Protes-
tantism--and between Wittenberg, Geneva and Rome. These
two disparate visions had set Luther and Calvin as fiercely
against the Täufer as the papists. [7] It was this polarization
(as Professor Allison has argued in The Rise of Moralism[8]
--an important if also biased study) that had produced two ri-
val traditions in Anglican theology and two centuries of stub-
born controversy. Bishop McAdoo has analyzed this same
phenomenon rather differently and in a much more richly nuanced argument (in The Spirit of Anglicanism). [9] Mutatis
mutandis, the live issue at the heart of the tumultuous controversies in the Roman Catholic Church--in Jansenism and
in the De Auxiliis battle--was not a speculative issue but the
question as to what it means to become and be a Christian.
This is one of the reasons why Vatican II was a landmark,
since it created a new climate in which to probe the ancient
problems of "grace and free will." The fourth world synod

of Catholic bishops in Rome focused on the theme "The Evangelization of the Modern World." If you set this against Bangkok, Lausanne and Jerusalem it becomes obvious that Christian evangelism and nurture is truly an ecumenical horizon.

It was Wesley--heir to the Protestant agony but rooted in an older, richer tradition of Scripture and tradition--who recognized more clearly than any other theologian of his time that the old Reformation polarities had ceased to define the Christian future (which is the score on which he surpasses Butler, whose mind was far more powerful). Thus--in the swirlings of the Revival and in reaction to its anomalies--Wesley conceived his theological vocation as the message of "faith alone" and "holy living," affirmed together in negation of all polarizations. It is in terms of his success and failure in this attempt--and in whatever sense we can say that this attempt is still relevant to us--that we may speak of Wesley's "place" in the Christian tradition.

Almost from the beginning, of course, there were shrewd observers who realized that Wesley was into a theological juggling act that might well come to no good end. In 1742, the bright young vicar of All Saints, Bristol (Josiah Tucker) commented on the instabilities he perceived in Wesley's teachings and the confusions they were creating. [10] From September, 1745, to March, 1748, a friendly critic signing himself "John Smith" (almost certainly not a bishop) tried to help Wesley see that his doctrine of "palpable inspiration" was incompatible with his avowed catholic views of grace, the means of grace, and the meaning of sacramental community. Wesley politely rejected their counsel[11]--he really never learned much from critics--and argued instead that there was already proof enough that "faith alone" and "holy living" could actually be held together, and were being held together--in the experience of the Methodist Christians! In this same early period Wesley broke with Whitefield because of his one-sided stress on sola fide--and then with William Law for precisely the opposite emphasis. Wesley turned on the Establishment--symbolized for him by Bull, Tillotson, et al. --accusing them of placing moral resolution ("works") ahead of "faith alone. " He forfeited the B. D. degree (that, as Fellow of Lincoln, he was morally obligated to take) because of a "supposition speech" that is, clearly, one of the worst sermons he ever wrote: the Latin is elegant but the spirit is uncharitable, hypocritical and reckless.[12]

As the Revival wore on it was the Calvinist remnant in the Church of England that offered Wesley his sternest challenge. Moreover, the battle-lines between them were defined by the old distinction between the "causes" of justification--"formal" versus "meritorious. " The debate on this point runs back at least to Frith and Gardiner, Cartwright and Hooker, Whitaker and Baro, Davenant and Thomas Jackson, et al. Finally, in 1765, Wesley took his stand (in "The Lord Our Righteousness")--affirming Christ's death as the meritorious cause of our justification, denying it as formal cause. Five years later, he shattered the uneasy truce with a theological "minute" on justification in and for his annual Conference. My first impression of this "minute" was that it was carelessly drafted (it is lacking in nuance!). More lately, however, I've come to believe that Wesley meant to provoke the Calvinists--as indeed he did. Subsequently, he was willing to mitigate his offense but not to retract his offending views. Otherwise, he would not have published Fletcher's "vindication"[13] when it might so easily have been suppressed --nor unleashed Walter Sellon and Thomas Olivers on the

predestinarians.[14] It is simply untrue that Wesley ever
abandoned the sola fide--but it is likewise undeniable that, after 1770, his stress was on "holy living" in opposition to its
distortions (as he saw them) by the other evangelicals. It is
no accident that his first great sermon ("The Circumcision
of the Heart," 1732-33) and his last great one ("The Wedding
Garment," 1790) bracketed a life-long plea: for the love of
God above all else and the love of all else in God.

The "interim" between this "beginning" and "end" de-
fies simple narration, for it involves an elaborate analysis
of Wesley's sources and his use of them. On this score he
is downright unhelpful, largely (one supposes) because he saw
no need for documentation (save from Scripture) for his particular readers. What is required, therefore (and what has
yet to be done adequately, by my lights at least), is a reading of Wesley against what Wesley himself read, with a view
to some sort of form-critical history of his sources and editorial procedures--as in his sermons, the Journal, The
Christian Library and The Arminian Magazine, etc. This is
a job that I've begun but not finished (and now may never)--
and space is too limited here for more than some core-
samplings from an incomplete exploration. Even this, however, will illustrate what I mean by trying to place Wesley
in his own times, on his own terms--within a critical historiographical perspective.

One place to begin is with the underestimated fact that
both his parents were converts to Anglicanism after their
careful upbringings in Nonconformity. There is a stereotype
of Samuel, Sr. as "self-seeking"--of which it is enough to
say that either he was superlatively inept in his self-seeking
or else was sadly self-deceived. He was inept--and eccen-
tric and a born loser--but his prime motives were stubborn-

ly principled, and those principles were Tory Anglicanism, but-
tressed by that horror of further anarchy from Nonconformity
that had triggered his first conversion. How else explain his
quixotic defense of Henry Sacheverell, or Bishop Atterbury, or
his reckless attacks upon the Dissenters? Susanna Annesley's
Anglican conversion was more reflective but no less painful--
the youngest daughter of Nonconformity's great patriarch, moving from Dissent to its other verge. John Wesley was bred up--
in this climate of unrewarded virtue--to a theological position
not fairly labeled "Arminian" or "Laudian" and certainly not
"latitudinarian." It was, instead, what Peter Heylyn had already described and defended as "the old English Protestantism"--older than Dort and Arminius, older than Henry
VIII. [15] The elder Wesleys understood this as a gospel of
moral rectitude (the prevailing Anglican view at the time) and
John imbibed it, even as he was learning the craft of preaching from his father (including a code of abbreviations). From
Susanna he had learned the essence of will-mysticism (Cas-
tañiza-Scupoli and Scougal). [16] From both Susanna and Samuel, Sr. he had come by his lifelong aversion to predestination.

    At Charterhouse and Christ Church he experienced a
basic reorientation (what I'd call a "conversion," as does
Webster's Dictionary)--to the tradition of Christian humanism, twin-rooted as it was in the classics and the Scriptures.
His later disparagements of his formal education need to be
weighed against the obvious fact that it bore him a lifetime
harvest of information, insights and a characteristic rhetoric
(his comments about "plain words for plain people" to the
contrary notwithstanding).

    In 1725, he was converted yet again--this time to the
existential import of the "holy living" traditions of his child-

hood and adolescence (this, plainly, is what he is trying to
tell us in § 2 of the successive editions of his Plain Account
of Christian Perfection).[17] If a man is entitled to but one
"conversion" in his lifetime (as the pietists insist), this
wasn't it.   But its burden ("holy living") became as profound
an element in his continuing Christian concerns as sola fide
did after 1738.   Incidentally, Wesley claimed later that, at
this stage of his Christian development, he had never heard
of the sola fide,[18] but this is hyperbole, to say the least.
We know that, later, he alludes to almost every issue in the
great debates that had been triggered by Dort and TULIP, to
the antinomianism of John Saltmarsh and Tobias Crisp (solifidianism run wild), to Bull, Baxter and Bunyan.   We also
know that he turned to Cranmer (in 1738) for validation of
his "new" theology and that in 1744 he had his preachers read
Baxter's Aphorisms on Justification (1640)--a scarce item
even then, since Baxter had already disowned it.[19] Did
Wesley learn all this after Aldersgate?   Of course not; not
even poor lectures at Oxford could have failed to orient him
toward this notorious past.   And even in his own time there
were men like John Guyse (1680-1761) and Philip Doddridge
(1702-1751).   What Wesley meant was that, until his confrontations by the Moravians and Salzburgers, he had never
been challenged by sola fide as a personal demand for decision.   The aftermath of this confrontation--Peter Böhler, Aldersgate, Herrnhut, Jonathan Edwards' Faithful Narrative of
a Surprising Work of God in New England (published in 1736,
but not read by Wesley until October of 1738)--makes clear,
good sense, and it adds up to a twin conclusion: 1738 was
Wesley's theological annus mirabilis and Aldersgate was the
dramatic moment in that year when he reversed the priorities
between sola fide and holy living, never to reverse them again.

It is, however, gravely misleading to suppose that Aldersgate settled Wesley's mind or stabilitized his subsequent reflections. He was, by instinct, a reactor--and the unfoldings of an unscripted religious movement kept him in much more of a theological turmoil than he ever confessed to--although its signs are abundant, once noticed. The Moravians realized this quickly and fenced him from their communion as homo perturbatus. [20] Then there are those brief apertures into his recurring religious despair--as recorded, for example, in the Journal for January 4, 1739, or in that letter to Charles, June 27, 1766. [21] More important was his quiet abandonment of his early equation of justification with assurance that drove so many people into hysterical despair. [22] Then there was the epidemic (at Colne, and elsewhere, in the '60s) of profession of entire sanctification as a "second blessing"--Wesley's acceptance of these "facts" and the adjustments in his theoretical accountings for them. Finally, there were the changes forced on him in his struggles with the Moravians and the Calvinists.

One way to comment on these various deviations from the trajectory that had been set for him at Aldersgate is that, although Wesley had finally got the sola fide in its proper and prime place in the mystery of salvation, he was simply unwilling to abandon his holy living motif or assimilate it to sola fide, as the Calvinists had done:

> We need [Beza had said] not use the slightest labour to determine whether this one or that [justification or sanctification] precedes in order, since we never receive the one without the other.... [23]

This meant, in effect, that Wesley rejected each of the classical Protestant formulations of sola fide, since none of them allowed for his doctrine of perfection and the expec-

tation of being perfected in love in this life.[24] In their place
he developed a soteriology based in part on classical Augus-
tinian foundations (Christology, original sin, etc.) but that
evangelized the Christian ethic and moralized the Christian
evangel, that linked justification with regeneration, that affirmed both the imputation and impartation of righteousness,
that repudiated both human self-assertion and passivity.   He
turned out "rules" by the dozen--but also with warnings that
even the most scrupulous rule-keeping will get you only to
the state of being an "almost Christian."   He developed intensive small group nurture and therapy for Christian matur-
ation (as Professor Oden has so shrewdly noticed).[25]   But
all of these were elements in his larger project: to describe
and promote the Christian life as rooted in faith and fruiting
in love.

He intimates as much, in a tantalizing report of his
activities for the week of November 12-18, 1738:

> Sunday, November 12 -- I preached at the Castle
> (Oxford). In the following week I began more nar-
> rowly to inquire what the doctrine of the Church of
> England is concerning the much-controverted point
> of justification by faith; and the sum of what I found
> in the Homilies I extracted and printed for the use
> of others.[26]

This is a strange understatement.   The obvious reference here
is to the Homilies and the Articles, and to a resultant
pamphlet (Wesley's first theological charter), The Doctrine of
Salvation, Faith and Good Works According to the Church of
England (1738).   But this agenda by itself would not have
busied Wesley for a full week.   The Homilies and Articles
had complex backgrounds and then there were the debates
that followed.   There was the further fact that Wesley knew
(as everyone else knew) that the doctrine of the Church of

England on "this much-controverted" point had never reached
consensus.

   The Homilies--at least those decisive for Wesley--
meant Cranmer, and back of Cranmer there was Martin Bu-
cer (with his doctrine of _iustitia duplex_ and his conciliatory
formulae in The Regensburg Book [1541]), with Gropper and
Contarini.   Also back of Cranmer was Melanchthon (and his
causa concurrens)--plus the not so incidental fact that Cranmer's father-in-law was Andreas Osiander.   Still further back
was the fountainhead of Christian humanism in England:
Erasmus; and back of him, the free will traditions of English
nominalism (_facere quod in se est_)[27] plus the "holy living"
mysticisms of Richard Rolle and Juliana of Norwich.

   The Articles were the Anglican bastion for the sola
fide tradition and had been construed by the Calvinists as an
official sanction for their famous "five points": TULIP. But
Wesley knew that this predestinarian interpretation of the Articles had in fact been declined by the majority of Anglican
divines in the seven decades following the collapse of the
Puritan Commonwealth. He had, therefore, an interesting
exercise: working his way back through this thicket (from
Edwards to Juliana) and then deciding to abridge Cranmer's
matchless rhetoric and use it as piling for his own position.
Here, then, was an Anglican who was prepared to surrender
the Anglican cause against the Puritans and Dissenters on
many counts (prelacy, vestments, a settled clergy dependent
on secular support, etc.). He was also on the threshold of
taking up the Täufer tradition of field preaching and intensive
small group discipline.[28] Even "the world is my parish" bit
was an old Täufer motto.[29] And yet he was still a staunch
and self-conscious Anglican, determined to graft his evangelical message onto its Anglican rootstock. He rejected popery

but went still further--rejecting sacerdotalism even as he
sought to develop a complex doctrine of sacramental grace
consonant with Hooker's Laws of Ecclesiastical Polity, V.
He would presently wear out his welcome at St. Mary's, Oxford, but would continue accepting his Lincoln stipend without
any quid pro quo.   He would denounce the Establishment and
nearly all its works, pass sweeping judgments against its
priesthood and universities, give the bishops of Exeter and
Gloucester the back of his hand--and still hold his Methodist
people within the Church of England even after their separation was virtually predetermined.   One might guess that there
was a tacit agreement amongst the English bishops (or was it
just their weakness?) to avoid a shootout with the Methodists
(apart from local troubles, etc.).   Thus the Methodist mission still continued largely in and for the Church of England--
as Richard Graves recognizes, satirically, in his Spiritual
Quixote:

> Our modern itinerant reformers are acting in defi-
> ance of human laws, without any apparent necessity
> of any divine commission.   They are planting the
> gospel in a Christian country.... [30]

Much has been made of Luther's "preface" to the Romans as the stimulus for Wesley's heartwarming at Aldersgate.   Less has been made of Wesley's subsequent strictures
on Luther's Commentary on Galatians[31] and on his deficient
doctrine of sanctification.

> Who has wrote more ably than Martin Luther on
> justification by faith alone?   And who was more ig-
> norant of the doctrine of sanctification, or more
> confused in his conceptions of it?[32]

Where Luther and Wesley are furthest apart is on the double
point of invincible concupiscence and "sin in believers"; this

is further correlated with their differences as to an expectation of Christian perfection in this life.

As for Wesley and Calvin, there was the repeated claim (sincere, I think) that, on the point of justification, Wesley stood no further than a hair's breadth from the Genevois. [33] And there is no doubt that Wesley came close to the Calvinist hard line on point T of TULIP: "total depravity and original sin." But he never seriously considered any of the other four points. Prevenience always seemed to him a more fruitful notion than election; universal redemption was a clear choice over limited atonement; he could never understand how grace could be irresistible or perseverance final. There was even a therapeutic side to his doctrine of God's lost image in sinful man so that the possibility of its restoration (therapeia psyches) remained, even in his fallen state. Instead of sin being rooted in the passions, Wesley saw it stemming from the will: it was defined, therefore, as "a violation of a known law of God."[34] The noisy gong between Wesley and the Calvinists was the doctrine of predestination, but the deeper issue between them was the seemingly fine point of Christ's atoning death being either the formal or the meritorious cause of justifying faith. Trent had distinguished five "causes of justification":

1. Final cause: the glory of God
2. Efficient cause: God's gratuitous mercy
3. Meritorious cause: Christ's passion and death
4. Instrumental cause: baptism
5. Formal cause: the conferred justice of God. [35]

The Puritans, following William Perkins' lead, [36] promptly misconstrued Trent's 5th point as meaning the infusion of an inherent human righteousness--which, of course, was "works-righteousness"! In opposition, therefore, they in-

sisted that Christ's death was the formal cause of our justi-
fication--from which the TULIP syndrome followed as a logical consequence, since formal causes are efficacious by definition and it is self-evident that Christ's death is not efficacious in all.

The Anglican reply (and it had to be cautious, lest it
appear to agree with Trent!) was that justification's formal
cause is God's covenanting mercy to all who believe. But
this allows the affirmation of Christ's death as meritorious
cause (cf. Trent's point #3!). After a quarter century of
preaching the sola fide in a way that included imputation and
impartation, relative and real changes, justification and regeneration, etc., Wesley felt constrained to formulate this
position, as we mentioned, in "The Lord Our Righteousness."

This (and that 1770 "minute") meant that Wesley's last
two decades were caught up in a constant polemic carried to
the point of tedium and overkill. Its tone is reflected in the
title of Wesley's house organ that he forged as his prime weapon
in the war: The Arminian Magazine (1778). This title represents a defiant acceptance of a pejorative label that the Calvinists had pinned on him (like "Methodist" back at Oxford)--
an epithet they hurled at most of their opponents. Laud was
an "Arminian," but so, too, were Hales and Montague and
even Baxter! Thus, Wesley became an "Arminian"--chiefly
in the sense that he had never been a Calvinist! But he
might also have been called a "Baxterian" (with as much or
little precision) and, in any case, his "Arminianism" was not
learned from Arminius himself, certainly not in his formative years. Arminius does not appear in The Christian Library,[37] where Wesley parades most of his theological favor-
ites. In The Arminian Magazine we have Peter Bertius' fu-
neral sermon,[38] and a pro-Remonstrant history of Dort[39]--

and that is all.

What we do find in this polemical arsenal is a fantastic panel of ancient witnesses to the old debates of which we have been speaking, some of them so obscure, to us, that one wonders wherever Wesley could have found them. There are, for example, Thomas Goad, Samuel Hoard, John Plaifere, Laurence Womock, et al. (from the English side) and Sebastian Castellio from the continent--all advocates of free will and "holy living." I offer you Plaifere and Castellio as two samples from a dozen: they are representative and have been ignored (as far as I know) by Wesley scholars. If I'm mistaken on this point, a friendly correction would be welcome.

John Plaifere is so obscure that he fails to show in the DNB--and has only one entry in the B.M. Cat. and the McAlpin Collection.[40] But this one item, Appello Evangelium (1651), turns out to be a very interesting essay--all the more so when you consider its appearance at the zenith of Puritan power. It argues for "the true doctrine of divine predestination concorded with the orthodox doctrine of God's free grace and man's free will"--and is self-consciously Erasmian. What is even more unexpected (and significant) is that when Wesley--a ruthless abridger--comes to a long quotation in Plaifere on justification (from a century-old volume entitled A Necessary Doctrine and Erudition for Any Christian Man [1543]), he leaves that particular passage almost intact. Some of you will recognize, of course, that this Necessary Doctrine... is the so-called "King's Book" (of Henry VIII) and that one of the chief drafters of the article on justification was probably Stephen Gardiner--a staunchly Catholic bishop supporting a stubbornly Catholic king in a hot dispute with the pope (a frequent occurrence in medieval Europe). Plaifere's quotation appears in The Arminian Magazine in Volume

I, pp. 545-49; in the Lacey edition of The King's Book (1932)
the same passage runs from pp. 147-51--and argues for a
view of justification recognizably similar to that of Cardinal
Pole's at Trent. [41] What are we supposed to make of all
this?

Maybe even stranger is Wesley's 100-page-plus selec-
tion (in volumes IV [1781] and V [1782]) of Sebastian Castellio's "Dialogues on Predestination, Election and Free Will"
(1st edition, 1578). Castellio [Chatefllon] may be familiar
to you as an elegant Latinist, translator of Scripture and à
Kempis, a famous raconteur of Bible stories and an ardent
advocate of religious toleration. But only Buisson has attempted a substantive discussion of these theological dia-
logues--and not very perceptively, either. Wesley seems to
have discovered them in a volume published in Frankfurt in
1696 in which four dialogues (#IV. De fide) were bound together with a translation of the De Imitatione Christi--from
monkish to Ciceronian Latin ("è latino in latinum"). Wesley
wanted this text of à Kempis for his scholars at the Kingswood School. But he must also have noticed an "address to
the reader" in it by none other than Faustus Socinus! He
may or may not have known that Castellio's Dialogues had
been denounced by Sir Francis Knollys to Lord Burleigh and
the Earl of Leicester and then suppressed by Queen Eliza-
beth. [42] This is why I find his introduction so intriguing:

> Numberless treatises have been written, in this
> and the last age, on the subject of Predestination:
> but I have not seen any that is written with more
> good sense and good humour, than Castellio's Dia-
> logues, wrote above two hundred years ago. Yet
> I know not that they have ever appeared in our
> tongue. I believe, therefore, the putting them in-
> to an English dress will give pleasure to every
> impartial reader. [43]

What were readers to make of Castellio, or we, of Wesley's interest, or of Wesley's as the only English translation printed?

What this shows is that Wesley had an immense bibliography under review (rarely the famous titles, either--or the ones that have come down to us as "famous"). He had analyzed these old controversies with skill and shrewdness and had chosen his options in accordance with a self-chosen image he was willing for the world to see (if any would take the trouble to notice his unadvertised clues). It is the image of an Anglican folk-theologian, a mass-evangelist, a small-group therapist, whose message was faith working by love leading to holiness. This central vision is clear and its exposition is far more richly nuanced than any of his interpreters (as far as I know them) have seemed yet to realize. What is more, after checking the roster of Wesley's colleagues in the history of Christian thought, I find very few of them (saving always the handful of speculative geniuses) who have surpassed or even matched his grasp of theology as a scientia practica.

Over the course of Christian thought about the mystery of salvation--to venture a glittering generality that covers a multitude of analytic sins--one may see two great contrasting perspectives. They have always been in unstable tension and when either has succeeded in obscuring the other, the results have been debilitating. One has been more largely associated with what we have come to call Latin Christianity; the other is more characteristically Eastern and Greek. The code words, in Latin Christianity, have been "pardon," "acquittal," "remission," "final glory," etc.; in Greek Christianity: "forgiveness," "reconciliation," "participation," "perfection." Latin Christianity has been dominated by forensic images, metaphors from the law courts (Roman and

medieval); Greek Christianity has been fascinated by visions
of ontological "participation in God": metousia theou.   One
stresses the Cross; the other points to the Cross but also
past it, to the glory beyond.   No theologian worth the label
has ever denied either of these emphases outright--but the
historian who cannot see and feel the radical differences in
tonality between the two traditions (without explaining them
away by references to politics, etc.) is strangely insensitive.
And yet, one of the capital features of our own new ecumenical age--tragically crippled as we are in the present moment with a near total collapse of practical statesmanship in
the movement--is the mutual interaction of Western and Eastern theologies and theologians and the consequence for our
newer views and experiences of Christian spirituality.   This
means, at the very least, that any Protestant theologian who,
by intention and partial achievement, has grasped the vital
unity of both Pardon and Participation motifs is at least as
relevant for our times as most other spokesmen for more
disjunctive systems--and more relevant than our current
fashion-mongers of the so-called "new theologies."   Wesley,
in my judgment, grasped this vital unity firmly, and this is
what gives him his distinctive "place"--then and now.

For classical Protestantism--to put no finer point on
it--has been dominated by the forensic-pardon theme of
"rightwising," in conscious contrast to all forgiveness-partici-
pation themes.   Roman Catholicism has maintained the participation theme but has linked it with theories of sacramental action and a sacerdotal control of the means of grace
that marks it off from the patristic traditions of Irenaeus,
Gregory of Nyssa, Maximos the Confessor, et al.

Wesley inherited the participation-motif from Casta-
ñiza-Scupoli, de Renty, Gregory Lopez--even William Law--

before he discovered its primal sources in the Johannine
Gospel and its patristic interpreters (under the stimulus of
the patristic revival in Oxford that he joined in).   Thus,
"holy living" as a vision of Christian existence was his earliest orientation.   But there is a flaw in any such orientation
unless it is balanced off by a firm emphasis on sola fide
(sola Dei gloria!)--and this became the burden of Wesley's
bitter complaint against "the mystics"[44] before Aldersgate,
and frequently thereafter. [45]

But sola fide has its own inbuilt extremism--Wesley
denounced it as "solifidianism."[46]   This, in Lutheranism,
tended toward a dominance in the church by exegetes and
"dogmaticians" or else a move toward inwardness (pietism)
--and, in both, to one sort or another of political quietism
(cuius regio, and all that).   In the Reformed tradition, stress
on the sola fide tended to translate sovereign grace into sovereign fiat (election) and to envisage theocracy as a political
ideal (the divine right of the elect to rule!).

Wesley sought--and I think found--a third alternative
to these polarities in his concept of faith alone, working by
love, aimed at holy living: pardon in order to participation!
Salvation, he tirelessly proclaimed, is by grace, through
faith, unto those good works which God has prepared that we
should walk in them--acting out our love of God in love to
neighbor and all creation (cf. Eph. 2:8-10).   Does this faith
nullify the moral Law?   Mē genoitō! Much rather, we estab-
lish the law by faith. [47]   Moreover, faith is not an end in itself and therefore not an ultimate concern, not even in Til-
lich's sense.   Faith is in order to love, as love is in order
to blessedness, which is God's original design for his human
creatures.   The holy life (love as a pure intention) is the
happy life; no other is or can be, now or ever.   Thus, justi-

fication and sanctification are God's gifts received and shared
by faith, hope and love (these three and none by itself alone).
Wesley believed this and taught it--and this serves to "place"
him in the Christian tradition more firmly and significantly
than his undeniably great rôle as "founder of Methodism."

We may speak of the contemporary relevance of this
message and mission only in a postscript. The situation is
something like this, in my view. The issues of the 16th-
18th centuries are now no longer current, in their historic
modalities, save in the case of our still-living ancestors
whom we call "fundamentalists." The controversies between
Lutherans and Reformed, between the Anglicans and the Romans and the Täufer are simply passé, as far as the hori-
zons of contemporary theology may be scanned. And yet the
concerns that were advanced and defended in those controversies are still with us and require new problematic formulations in authentically ecumenical terms. The old ensigns--
sola fide, sola Scriptura, "holy church," "holy tradition" (all
"either/or")--are no longer rallying points for future theologizing. But still there is no assuagement for the pain and
emptiness and hunger of the human heart for a meaningful
life and a meaningful death--and there can be none apart from
God's sovereign grace gracefully received (what else was sola
fide all about, really?) or apart from "holy living" (God's
grace enabling human love to flower and fruit in happiness,
personal and communal). The old disjunction between "evangelical" and "catholic" is no longer a fruitful polarity and the
only conceivable Christian future is for a church truly catholic, truly evangelical and truly reformed. John Wesley--as
an evangelist with a catholic spirit, a reformer with a heroic
vision of the Christian life created by faith matured in love,
a theologian who lived in and thought out of the Scripture and

Christian tradition and who brought all his judgments to the
bar of experience and reason--this Wesley offers a treasure
to the church of tomorrow that will leave it the poorer if ignored.

The irony, of course, is that this thesis (right or
wrong) is not readily verifiable, since Wesley is not really
accessible, for want of proper, critical editions and compe-
tent studies from across the entire spectrum of ecumenical
scholarship.   The rescue of Wesley from his Methodist co-
coon and his neglect by non-Methodists was part of the original vision of the Oxford Edition of Wesley Works.   In my own
view, it is still the project's chief warrant and best hope.

NOTES

1. Cf. Luke Tyerman, The Life and Times of the Rev.
    John Wesley (New York: Harper & Brothers, 1872),
    Vol. I, p. 1.

2. The Making of the English Working Class (New York:
    Pantheon Books, 1964), pp. 41-46, 53-54, 362-64.

3. Bernard Semmel, The Methodist Revolution (New York:
    Basic Books, Inc., 1973; London: Heinemann Educa-
    tional Books Limited, 1974).

4. "The English heritage and the German contribution formed
    in John Wesley a true and authentic alliance." Martin
    Schmidt, John Wesley: A Theological Biography (Lon-
    don, 1962), Vol. I, p. 309.

5. Cf. Hubert Jedin, A History of the Council of Trent
    London, 1958), Vol. II, ch. v, pp. 166-196.

6. On this point, cf. Semmel, op. cit., ch. II, "The Battle
    Against 'Speculative' Antinomianism," pp. 23ff., and ch.
    III, "Confrontation with 'Practical' Antinomianism,"
    pp. 56ff.

7. Cf. John S. Oyer, Lutheran Reformers Against Anabap-

tists (The Hague, 1964), pp. 212, 234.

8. New York: Seabury Press, 1966.

9. New York: Charles Scribner's Sons, 1965.

10. A Brief History of the Principles of Methodism (Oxford,
    1742).

11. See The Principles of a Methodist. Occasioned by a
    late Pamphlet intitled, "A Brief History of the Prin-
    ciples of Methodism" (Bristol, 1742). For the "Smith-
    Wesley" correspondence in extenso, see Henry Moore,
    Life of the Rev. John Wesley (London: Kershaw,
    1825), Vol. II, pp. 473-576.

12. "Hypocrisy at Oxford," Isa. 1:21, June 27, 1741.
    Thomas Jackson published the English text of this ser-
    mon under the title, "The True Christianity Defended,"
    in The Works of John Wesley (London, 1872; Grand
    Rapids, Michigan: Zondervan, 1958), Vol. VII, pp.
    452-462. The Latin text--in Wesley's holograph--is
    in the Morley Collection, Wesley College, Bristol.

13. "A Vindication of the Rev. Mr. Wesley's Last Minutes:
    occasioned by a circular, printed letter, inviting prin-
    cipled persons, both clergy and laity ... to oppose
    them in a body...." Signed "J. F[letcher]. July 29,
    1771." [This was sponsored and edited by Wesley
    himself.]

14. Cf. Walter Sellon, "A Defence of God's Sovereignty...";
    "Arguments Against General Reprobation Considered";
    "An Answer to Aspasio Vindicated"; "Sermons on I
    Tim. 4:14 and Titus 3:5," in Works (London, 1814),
    2 vols. See also Thomas Olivers, "A Defence of
    Methodism: Delivered ... in a public debate ... held
    in London ... 1785, on the following question, Have
    the Methodists done most good or evil?" (Leeds,
    1818); "A full defence of Rev. John Wesley, in answer
    to several personal reflections cast on that gentleman
    by the Rev. Caleb Evans...." (London, 1776); "A
    full refutation of the doctrine of unconditional persever-
    ance: in a discourse on Hebrews" (London, 1790).

15. Cf. his Historia Quinquarticularis (London, 1681), Part
    III, ch. xxii, 631.

16. Cf. Juan de Castañiza [i.e., Lorenzo Scupoli], Spiritual
    Conflict, tr. by Robert Reade and revised by Richard
    Lucas (London, 1698); and Henry Scougal, The Life of
    God in the Soul of Man; or the Nature and Excellency
    of the Christian Religion, etc. (1677); 6th ed. with a
    preface by Gilburt Burnet (London, 1733).

17. A Plain Account of Christian Perfection, as Believed
    and Taught by The Reverend Mr. John Wesley, from
    the Year 1725, to the Year 1777, in Works, XI, 366-
    448. (Six editions were printed between 1766-1789.)

18. For example, cf. "Remarks on Mr. Hill's Review"
    (Works, X, 403): "...I did not see clearly that we
    are saved by faith till the year 1738." Also his letter
    to William Law, in The Letters of John Wesley, (ed.)
    John Telford, Vol. I, pp. 239-242, dated May 14,
    1738, where Wesley sharply criticizes his old mentor
    for not having "advised" him of "this living, justifying
    faith in the blood of Jesus." In his "Farther Appeal
    ..." (Works, VIII, 111), Wesley says he was ordained
    deacon in 1725 and "during all that time I was utterly
    ignorant of justification and confounded by sanctifica-
    tion...." In one of his last sermons, "On the Wed-
    ding Garment," § 18 (Works, VII, 317), he says, "On-
    ly about fifty years ago [i.e., 1738-40] I had a clearer
    view than before of justification by faith--and in this
    time, from that very hour, I never varied...."

19. And had not authorized its second (last) printing in 1649.

20. Cf. Daniel Benham (ed.), Memoirs of James Hutton
    (London, 1856), p. 40.

21. Cf. The Journal of John Wesley, (ed.) Nehemiah Curnock,
    Vol. II, p. 125, and Letters, V, 14-16. See also Al-
    bert C. Outler (ed.), John Wesley in A Library of
    Protestant Thought (New York: Oxford University
    Press, 1964), pp. 80-82.

22. Cf. Bernard G. Holland, " 'A Species of Madness': The
    Effect of John Wesley's Early Preaching," in Wesley
    Historical Society Proceedings, Vol. XXXIX, Part 3
    (October, 1973), pp. 77-85, and especially pp. 81-85.

23. Cf. William Forbes, Considerationes Modestae et Pa-
    cificae (1658), in A Library of Anglo-Catholic Theol-

ogy (1850), Vol. I, p. 173.

24.   Cf. "The Large Minutes," 1766, p. 54.

25.   Thomas Oden, The Intensive Group Experience: The
      New Pietism (Philadelphia: The Westminster Press,
      1972), pp. 56-88.

26.   Journal, II, 101.

27.   Cf. Wesley's Oxford Diary, V, [vi]:   "Q?   How steer
      between Scrupulosity, as to particular instances of
      Self Denial, and Self-indulgence?   A. Fac quod in te
      est, & Deus aderit bonae tuae Voluntati."   Cf. also
      the sermons, "On Working Out Our Own Salvation,"
      III. 6-7 (Works, VI, 512-513); "The Signs of the
      Times," II.10 (Works, VI, 311); "The General Spread
      of the Gospel," § 9 (Works, VI, 280); "The Imperfec-
      tions of Human Knowledge," § 1 (Works, VI, 337);
      "On Schism," § 21 (Works, VI, 410).   Knowledge,
      § 1 (Works, VI, 337); "On Schism," § 21 (Works, VI,
      410).
          See also Heiko A. Oberman, Harvest of Medieval
      Theology (Cambridge, Massachusetts: Harvard Univer-
      sity Press, 1963), pp. 129-45, and my chapter,
      "Methodism's Theological Heritage: A Study in Per-
      spective," in Methodism's Destiny in an Ecumenical
      Age, edited by Paul Minus, Jr. (New York: Abingdon
      Press, 1969), pp. 52-60.
          For a sample of Luther's consistent rejection of
      this in se est tradition, cf. Table Talk, in Works
      (1967), Vol. 54, p. 392.

28.   For a reference to field preaching and "Corner Preach-
      ers," cf. Oyer, op. cit., p. 128.   Wesley never ad-
      mits this lineage but the plaques on Hanham Mount
      make it clear enough.   They read (1) "Out of the
      Wood Came Light"; (2) "Dedicated to the Field Preach-
      ers, 1658-1739"; (3) "From 1658-1684 persecuted
      Bristol Baptist preachers preached in Hanham Woods
      to the people of this neighbourhood.   The preachers
      often swam the flooded Avon and risked imprisonment
      and death for their faith."   Whitefield and Wesley were
      following in their train!

29.   Cf. Franklin Littell, "The Anabaptist Theology of Mis-
      sions," in The Mennonite Quarterly Review, Vol.

XXI, No. 1 (January, 1947), p. 12.

30. The Spiritual Quixote; Or, the Summer's Ramble of Mr.
     Geoffry Wildgoose (1773) [Barbauld Edition, London,
     1820], Vol. I, p. 55.

31. Cf. Journal, II, 467.

32. "On God's Vineyard," I.5 (Works, VII, 204).

33. Cf. "Minutes of the Second Annual Conference, Bristol,
     Thursday August 1, 1745," Question 22f. in LPT
     Wesley, op. cit., pp. 151-152. See also Wesley's
     letter to John Newton, May 14, 1765 (Letters, IV,
     298).

34. Cf. "On Perfection," II.9; III.9 (Works, VI, 417, 423);
     see also Wesley's letter to John Hosmer, June 7,
     1761 (Letters, IV, 155).

35. Cf. Schaff, Creeds of Christendom, Vol. II, pp. 94-95:
     "Of this justification the causes are these: the (1)
     final cause indeed is the glory of God and of Jesus
     Christ, and the life everlasting; while the (2) efficient
     cause is a merciful God who washes and sanctifies
     gratuitously, signing, and anointing with the Holy Spir-
     it of promise, who is the pledge of our inheritance;
     but the (3) meritorious cause is his most beloved only-
     begotten, our Lord Jesus Christ, who, when we were
     enemies ... merited justification for us by his most
     holy Passion ... and made satisfaction for us unto
     God the Father; the (4) instrumental cause is the sac-
     rament of baptism, ... lastly, (5) the sole formal
     cause is the justice of God, not that whereby he him-
     self is just, but that whereby he maketh us just,
     whereby we ... are renewed in the spirit of our mind,
     and we are not only reputed, but are truly called, and
     are just, receiving justice within us, each one accord-
     ing to his own measure, which the Holy Ghost distrib-
     utes to every one as he wills, and according to each
     one's proper disposition and co-operation."   There is
     no word of inherent righteousness, apart from grace,
     in this text or none can rightly be derived from it.

36. Cf. William Perkins, A Golden Chaine, or The Descrip-
     tion of Theologie; Containing the Order of the Causes
     of Salvation and Damnation, According to God's Word.
     ... London, 1591.

37. Although we have Sir Henry Wotton's biography (with a
     character sketch of Arminius) in Vol. XV, pp. 342ff.

38. Cf. Vol. I (1778), pp. 9-17.

39. Ibid., pp. 17-28; 49-58; 97-107; 145-154.

40. Appello Evangelium [An Appeal to the Gospel] for the
     true doctrine of the Divine Predestination, concorded
     with the orthodox doctrine of God's free-grace, and
     man's free-will.... London, 1651.

41. Cf. Jedin, op. cit., II, 172, 181, 189.

42. Cf. Ferdinand Buisson, Sébastien Castellion: sa vie et
     son oeuvre (1515-1563) (Nieuwkoop: B. de Graff,
     1964), Appendice cxviii, Vol. II, p. 498.

43. The Arminian Magazine, Vol. IV, p. vi. Cf. also
     Works, XIV, 289.

44. Tuesday, January 24, 1738, Journal, I, 420. Cf. also
     his letter to his brother Samuel, November 23, 1736
     (Letters, I, 207).

45. Cf. Journal, III, 18, 241. See also Letters, V, 341;
     VI, 44.

46. Cf. Journal, II, 174; "Predestination Calmly Consid-
     ered," Works, X, 266f.; also Works, XIV, 231.

47. Cf. sermons XXXIV, "The Original, Nature, Property,
     and Use of the Law," XXXV, "The Law Established
     Through Faith, I," and XXXVI, "The Law Established
     Through Faith, II" (Works, V, 433-466).

CHAPTER II

SON OF SAMUEL:
JOHN WESLEY, CHURCH OF ENGLAND MAN

Gordon Rupp

"John Wesley was not a man to be forgotten," said Alexander Knox, after a lifetime of reflection on the significance of the great friend of his youth.   And so, after two
hundred years, say all of us.   Some of us who are Methodist preachers are in private duty bound to praise famous
men and our father who begat us.   All of us from a sense
that John Wesley belongs to the whole Church and indeed to
all mankind, are concerned to appraise him against the background of critical theological and historical scholarship in
which the great new edition of Wesley's works will take its
place.

Most of what needs to be said has been said and written many times and there are no great areas left wholly un-
explored, save perhaps, as Professor Semmel's ingenious essay seems to indicate, less discussion of origins than of the
impact of the Revival on the late 18th and early 19th centuries.   All I can do is to offer one or two program footnotes
to the discussion, concerned rather with roots than fruits.
All historiography is selective but conscious selectivity is
perhaps a great betrayal.   Yet I do want to press one or two
points where Wesley himself seems to offer a corrective to

39

our present age, and to concentrate on certain continuities
between John Wesley and the Christian tradition into which
he was born and bred, and which he made his own, as a
Church of England Man. [1]

The century 1550-1660, or perhaps between the Mas-
sacre of St. Bartholomew and the Revocation of the Edict of
Nantes, might be labeled "the Age of Zeal" and John Wesley's
sermon "On Zeal" might in our time be published as "A
Word to a Militant."

> Nothing [he says] has done more disservice to re-
> ligion, or more mischief to mankind than a sort of
> zeal which has for several ages prevaled....
> Pride, covetousness, ambition, revenge, have in
> parts of the world slain their thousands: but zeal
> its ten thousands. [2]

He instances the deadly effects of the appeal to violence in
the so-called Wars of Religion. He goes on to deplore the
violence of the tongue, of religious bigotry and zeal for opinions, and he takes Hooper and Ridley to task for initiating the
great "surplice brabble"--

> O shame to man! I would as soon have disputed
> about a straw or a barley-corn. [3]

These things left terrible legacies and bred a vehe-
ment reaction: in Britain, the exclusion of the Nonconform-
ists and within the Church of England a division into parties
which has bedeviled all in later history. Paradoxically the
recent rejection of union with the Methodists may have its
roots in the period before Methodism was. In Northern Ireland there is a still more terrible and living memorial. In
the life of the nation there was the reaction against austerity
in a callous permissive society, a moral inflation where the
weakest went to the wall, the reaction against emotion and
devotion, against all that could be labeled "enthusiasm," the

splitting asunder of the wholeness of faith into disparate and often opposing strands of rationalism, moralism and mysticism.   Yet in one field, that of Christian spirituality, there was throughout this age a wonderful flowering, the blossoms and fruit of the seed sown in the first works of the Protestant and Catholic Reformation, in the great Lutheran hymns, the psalms and liturgies of the galleys and of the Desert in the Reformed Church in France, and the many-sided richness of Puritan and Caroline devotion in England, with, in Catholic Spain, Italy and France, a succession of saints and heroic sodalities unmatched in any period of Christian history.   It was into this rich and many-sided inheritance of "inward religion" that Susanna and Samuel Wesley bred their children. [4]

I do not at all dispute what has been said and written of the importance of the influence of the incomparable Susanna on her children, nor, in the main, what has been written of her relation to the Puritan tradition.   Still less would I deny what Robert Monk and John Newton have said about Puritan influences on John Wesley, or Professor Horton Davies about the affinities between early Methodism and Nonconformist wor-ship.   But after all, Susanna was the extreme high church member of the family, the Nonjuror.   When at the age of 13 Susanna revolted in her father's house and turned to the Church of England, she joined a party which rapidly became a sect.   The letters to Lady Yarborough which turned up in the 1950s remind us of a whole side of the Wesley family life of which we know almost nothing.   Susanna speaks of seeking the advice of "our divines," which implies some active association with groups of people.   At any rate the Nonjuring element brought positive stresses: the search for primitive Christianity, the concern for frequent, nay, constant communion, for the fasts and festivals of the Church.   These were

to persist and grow in the Holy Club and were more important than ephemeral and anachronistic notions of passive obedience, of divine right and of loyalty to the Stuart cause which
Susanna held very obstinately and which provoked her to en-
dure the famous family row (the infighting in the Wesley family awaits its book).

But when Samuel Wesley trudged from Stoke Newing-
ton to Oxford, and turned his back on the militant epigone of
the Calves Head Clubs, it was to become the very model of
a Church of England man, to live henceforth in the mid-
stream of its life: as a Convocation Man, as a polemic divine, in his business as theological correspondent to the
Athenian Society, in his constant reading of English divines,
as well as in his massive philological and Biblical studies.
It was by his example and encouragement that the Wesley
children, three boys and at least two girls, took to writing
poetry.

Obviously Susanna was left to bear the brunt of their
education, but this was the way of that age. Samuel Wesley
gadding off for unconscionable intervals in London, leaving
his wife to cope with the home as well as her continual preg-
nancies, was simply in line with the male chauvinism of the
age. John Worthington did the same before him, and John
Byrom did not even return home to Manchester when his baby
died. Both Susanna and Samuel were perhaps a little jealous
at this point: she of her husband's overwhelming and often
overbearing learning; he of her evidently superior powers of
communication, and there are signs that Samuel tried rather
irritably to muscle in on her correspondence with the boys.
But his own letters of spiritual counsel to the eldest Samuel
have very good sense in them. When Susanna quoted and discussed what she had read in her husband's books we forget

that it was Samuel who first discovered "the surprising thoughts" of M. Pascal; and when a young lady at Oxford turned John towards the "Imitation of Christ" it is Samuel who breaks in with the sounder comments and the reminder that the little work, so seminal in early Methodism, was his own "old companion and friend."[5]

It is Samuel who introduced them to M. de Renty, that figure who taps on the mind of John Wesley throughout the years like a family ghost, an entirely sanctified Old Jeffry. It is Samuel who intercepts the Holy Club as it journeys northward with facilities for frequent communion, and his treatise on Baptism which his son was to draw heavily upon in later years. Of course, it is easy to caricature Samuel Wesley: wherever John got his business sense, it was not from his Father. But the obstinate courage which could face violent hatred is not to be missed or despised--"I always look a mob in the face" is a trait of John which his Father learned in grim conflict with the Upland men of the Fens who destroyed his property and menaced his person. And that fine letter to the boys in Oxford--the great "Valde Probo"-- there were not many country parsons in that age who could applaud actions which might ruin their hopes of future prefer- ment. John Wesley always signs letters to his mother "Your dutiful son," and when once he added "and affectionate" he provoked her to ironic comment; yet he always signs himself to his Father "your dutiful and affectionate son."

If John withstood his father to his face in the sad af- fair of his sister Hetty, the matter ended in gruff tears and embraces from the old man, and there is no mistaking the pride and joy with which he acclaimed his son as Fellow of Lincoln. It was Samuel the failed poet, Samuel the failed Biblical expositor, Samuel the failed missionary whose ambitions were fulfilled in John and Charles Wesley. And on his death bed he it was who, if they had known it, gave them the final clue in their great treasure hunt--"The inward witness --the inward witness."

I do not wish to underrate the importance of emotion in Wesley's life or in that of the Revival. The religion of the heart spoke to the condition of the arid emotional desert of the age, as in our time the charismatic and Jesus movements may fulfil an emotional need which the churches have not met. Yet in our age, a volcanic, apocalyptic, 17th-century-like world, where on all sides irrationalism seems to triumph not least in the church, where men are beset by problems they cannot diagnose let alone solve, where it is not a question of controlling the present but the past which is alive--it is surely not enough for the Church simply to add another element of irrationalism. The John Wesley we need to hear is the author of an appeal to Men of Reason and Religion.

Samuel Wesley's "Advice to a Young Clergyman"[6] is an astonishing document which deserves a modern critical edition. Its massive program of theological learning and pastoral care would seem impossibly demanding were there not evidence that Samuel himself had mastered it, and John too, as a comparison with his own "Address to the Clergy" and the titles of his Christian Library reveal. Primary is the study of the sacred languages and auxiliary tongues of use in the study of the Bible. But there is a wider range of auxiliary study which many of his contemporaries would have condemned as profane learning:

> logic, history, law, pharmacy, natural and experimental philosophy, chronology, geography, mathematics, even poetry, music or any other parts of learning.[7]

The first three and a half years of a curate's spare time are
to be spent in Biblical and patristic studies. The patristic
studies of Samuel Wesley's day were less the devotional lec-
tio divina of the great Carolines and Puritans--like Lancelot
Andrewes, Robert Bolton who quotes Chrysostom, Augustine,
Bernard on every other page, as the historical appeal to the
authority of Fathers and Councils in the fight against Popery
and Deism, and the new critical investigations of authenticity
in the writings of Wake and Bull and Grabe, and the historical studies of Tillemont and Dupin. Neither Samuel nor his
sons were deeply read in St. Augustine. The next three and
a half years are to be spent in the study of the moderns,
that massive succession of English divines in the Establishment and in Dissent whose writings Wesley described as a
standing glory of the Church of England: each with some
pithy comment attached--"Isaac Barrow--strong, masculine
and noble"; "Cave's Primitive Christianity etc.--good books
for a Clergyman's Family"; and a just comment on the
preaching of Tillotson--over valued by the age of Parson
Woodforde but very much underrated in our time, "Archbishop Tillotson [who] brought the art of preaching to perfection:
had there been as much life as there is of politeness, and
generally of cool, clear, close reasoning and convincing argument."[8]

At the end of this prospectus, which would make a
modern theological student turn pale, he adds some sensible
comments:

> I do not think all these books absolutely necessary,
> however this general view will do you no harm and
> ... you may read what you please and leave the
> rest to cobwebs. [9]

But there were no cobwebs on John Wesley, and what-

ever young Mr. Hoole had made of them, his successor John
Wesley explored them for the remainder of his life.   This
may be seen in Wesley's own program of theological reading
in his "Address to the Clergy" (1756). [10]   It offended and
angered William Law, who denounced it:

> almost all of it empty babble, fitter for an old
> grammarian that was grown blear eyed in mending
> dictionaries than for one who had tasted of the pow-
> ers of the world to come.

Wesley took over from his Father the list of profitable auxiliary studies:

> Is not a knowledge of profane history, likewise, of
> ancient customs, of chronology and geography,
> though not absolutely necessary, yet highly expedi-
> ent? [11]

Logic came first in Samuel's list and it is Wesley's emphasis on it which must have angered William Law.

> one (whether art or science), although now quite un-
> fashionable, is necessary next, and in order to the
> knowledge of Scripture itself.   I mean logic.   For
> what is this, if rightly understood, but the art of
> good sense'--of apprehending things clearly, judging
> truly and reasoning conclusively?

Let the candidate for orders ask himself:

> Am I a tolerable master of the sciences?   Have I
> gone through the very gate of them, Logic?   If not,
> I am not likely to go much further when I stumble
> at the threshold.   Do I understand it so as to be
> ever the better for it?

> [Does it, he asks, enable us to read with profit
> Henry More, Isaac Newton, Malebranche and Euc-
> lid?]

> If I have not gone thus far I am a novice still, what
> have I been about ever since I came from school? [12]

What indeed? It had been remarked of little John as a child that he always asked the reason for things. At Oxford he lectured in Logic. In 1768 we find him writing to Joseph Benson at Kingswood:

> Logic you cannot crack without a Tutor: I must read it to Peter and you, if we live to meet. [13]

On at least two refresher courses for his preachers he took textbooks on logic and rhetoric as his theme. [14] In January 1788 his Diary shows him, at 85, spending four successive mornings studying Logic. [15] In his compendium of Logic, which he published for the instruction of his school at Kingswood and for his young assistants, he indicates two of his sermons as exemplifying the logical method. It is significant that they are the Sermon on the Means of Grace--against the irrationalism of the quietists; and the sermon on Enthusiasm --against fanaticism and delusion in religion. [16]

I am not arguing "John Wesley: Wittgenstein's spiritual Ancestor," though both men sensed the fundamental mystery of words and of human communication. Dr. Anscombe sums up the Tractatus Apologeticus by saying that Wittgenstein "saw the world looking at him with a face. Logic helped to reveal that face." [17]

If this be too high a comparison, there is a luminous essay by Dorothy Sayers on the "Lost Tools of Learning" in which she shows how words and the use of them and the right ordering of them are at the fundament of culture. Wesley regarded new words and slang as a compost heap; he did not, as we do, consider them the garden. And he would have made short shrift of our contemporary immersion in jargon, not least in the Ecumenical dialogue. In one of his splendid prefaces, which are Wesley at his best, he confesses:

> I could even now write ... floridly and rhetorical-
> ly...; but I dare not.... I dare no more write in
> a fine style than wear a fine coat.... Let who will
> admire the French frippery. I am still for plain,
> sound English. 18

As the Ordinal bade him, Wesley drew all his studies one
way, towards the Bible. "My ground is the Bible. Yes, I
am a Bible-bigot. I follow it in all things, both great and
small." 19 He read and studied as his father had taught him,
and he learned from him to abridge and condense books until
he could gut them as a fisherman guts fish.

He was a great borrower. If sometimes he reminds
us of Oscar Wilde when he said of an epigram, "I wish I had
thought of that!" and got the reply, "You will, Oscar, you
will!" he was no mere Autolycus and from his great memory
could always pull the apt quotation from Horace or Virgil,
Milton, Pope or Prior as well as too many perhaps from
lesser breeds without the law. And he kept up his reading
to the end. It is the old Wesley who said:

> I generally travel alone in my carriage and so con-
> sequently am as retired ten hours a day as if I
> were in a wilderness.... I never spend less than
> three hours (frequently ten or twelve) in the day
> alone.

His reading of history was wide if his interpretations
were quirky: too eager to back lost causes, to accept as
proven the innocence of Mary Queen of Scots or the good
looks of Richard III, he had a way of reading himself back
into Church history.

> I have doubted whether ... Montanus was not one
> of the holiest men in the second century. Yes, I
> would not affirm that the arch-heretic of the fifth
> century [Pelagius] ... was not one of the holiest
> men of that age, not excepting St. Augustine ...
> [who was] as full of pride, passion, bitterness,

censorious and as foul-mouthed to all who contra-
dicted him, as George Fox [!] himself. [20]

His Primitive Physic, his clinic, his innumerable bits
of medical advice, show how seriously he took himself as a
follower of the Great Physician.   His own interest in and accurate observation of his own symptoms link his Journals
with those of David Livingstone.   And he read the important
treatises as they came out, the works of Dr. Cheyne, Cado-
gan on the Gout (though he doubts the value of eating pickles)
and that tract of Dr. Wilson on the "Circulation of the Blood"
which led him to exclaim, "What are we sure of but the
Bible?"   About books of travel, geography and science he in-
termits credulity and scepticism:

> I read Mr. Huygens' Conjectures on the Planetary
> World. He surprised me.   I think he clearly
> proves that the moon is not habitable. ... I know
> the earth is.   Of the rest I know nothing. [21]

This was the culture of a man of parts.   But if you
will read his sermons and especially the second and third series, you will find that those were indeed auxiliary sciences
to the Bible, used, as Bede and Erasmus had counseled, to
illuminate the study and exposition of the Word.

I would not exaggerate Wesley's rationalism.   It was
for thirty years something I used to argue about with my
teacher and friend Norman Sykes, who wrote of the

> retrograde intellectual influence of the Evangelical
> Revival ... even John Wesley, despite his academic
> training and scholarly attitude was almost supersti-
> tious in his notions of special interventions of prov-
> idence and in his recourse to the expedient of the
> sortes liturgicae for the determination of problems
> ....   The theological and literary productions of
> the Evangelical Revival were of little importance or
> permanent value to the tradition of the 'ecclesia
> docens.'[22]

No doubt Wesley's controversial writings, his two
"Appeals," and "Letters to John Smith," and his sermon on
"The Case of Reason Impartially Considered," do not rank
with the great works of Warburton, Butler and Paley, but
Wesley's works were directly suited to the needs of the revival and to the perils which beset it, as well as to the vul-
nerabilities of his colleagues and assistants:

> Never more declaim, in that wild, loose ranting
> manner against this precious gift of God, acknowl-
> edge 'the candle of the Lord' which he hath fixed
> in our souls for excellent purpose. [23]

At any rate Norman Sykes' distinguished forerunner,
H. M. Gwatkin, claimed that John Wesley was one of the
sanest minds of the 18th century.

The comments by Alexander Knox on Southey's _Life
of Wesley_ are among the best things ever written about him,
and he has an interesting comment on Wesley's mind and his
propensity for quick decision:

> He had an intellectual frame of singular construc-
> tion.... His habits of reflection bore no propor-
> tion to his quickness of apprehension; nor could he
> endure delay either in reasoning or acting. From
> uncertain and scanty premises he rapidly formed
> the most confident and comprehensive conclusions,
> mistaking logic for philosophy in matters of theory,
> and appearances for realities in matters of fact and
> experience.

Knox adds:

> I ... think he would have been an enthusiast if he
> could. He was always gratified by hearing or read-
> ing of illapses, or raptures, or supposed extraordi-
> nary manifestations, when he was assumed of the
> moral rectitude of the party;... But while he thus
> delighted in the soarings of others, he himself
> could not follow them in their flights: there was
> a firmness in his intellectual texture which would
> not bend to illusion. [24]

The modern church, like some elements in the Revival proceeds like the White Knight in "Alice" by a series of crashes, first on one side and then on another (the technical phrase is polarity). But Wesley kept his balance and when occasionally he fell, invariably he landed on his feet! We might almost speak of Wesley's Razor--that fine edge of the balance of truth. When we look at the first Minutes of the Conference we find him and his preachers aware of the risk of truth--like naughty little boys hanging over a cliff edge and seeing who could lean out furthest without disaster:

> Have we not ... leaned too much towards Calvinism?
> It seems we have.
>
> Have we not also leaned towards Antinomianism?
> We are afraid we have.
>
> . . . .
> Does not the truth of the Gospel lie very near both
> to Calvinism and Antinomianism?
> Indeed it does; as it were, within a hair's breadth.
> Wherein may we come to the very edge of Calvin-
> ism?[25]

Like a razor cutting to "within a hair's breadth," to "the very edge."

Hence, too, the delicate balance between Wesley's "inward religion" and mystical quietism and theosophy. Of this the Christian Library is the best evidence. Behind the catholicity, the diversity of movements from which the volumes are drawn, what matters is the unity into which Wesley drew them. They did not so much contribute to his mind as he took the Methodism out of theirs, their inner core of devotion and edification, "Scriptural Holiness." Many of these obvious devotional strands have been analyzed in recent years: Professor Outler on the Apostolic and the Greek Fathers, Professor Orcibal on the borrowings from Poiret, Antoinette

de Bourignon, Fenelon, Mme. Guyon and the Spanish Molinos
and John of Avila, the Nonjurors and the Scottish mystical
divines. Others have stressed the great representation of
Puritan works. Nor must we forget that when Wesley was
charged with making of it "an odd collection of mutilated writings of Dissenters of all sorts" he replied that "in the first
ten volumes there is not a line from any Dissenter of any
sort; and the greatest part of the other forty is extracted
from Archbishop Leighton, Bishops Taylor, Patrick, Ken,
Reynolds, Sanderson and other ornaments of the Church of
England. "[26]

Here I would comment on another remark of Alexander Knox:

> His standard of Christian virtue was pure and ex-
> alted. He formed his views in the school of the
> Greek Fathers, and in that of their closest modern
> followers, the Platonic divines of the Church of
> England. [27]

As a Fellow of Emmanuel College, Cambridge, I draw
attention to the fact that the Christian Library contains extracts from the writings of at least eight members of the college, Puritans, Platonists and Church of England men: John
Preston, William Bedell, Joseph Hall, John Worthington,
Ralph Cudworth, John Smith, Nathaniel Culverwell and William Law.

Perhaps only at Merton and Balliol in the 14th and
Oriel in the 19th century, at Oxford, has a religious crisis
emerged within a single college, such as the head-on generation clash within Emmanuel College between the Puritans and
their Platonist successors. What began as a discussion between students and tutors in the 1630s continued between
senior and younger dons in the '40s and exploded in the

1650s when the young men were becoming Heads of Houses,
finding public expression in the famous set-to between Andrew
Tuckney and Benjamin Whichcote.

Continuity is almost more significant than the conflict,
for both sets of men were scholars of great learning. Both
were grounded in the sacred languages and in the Bible and
in the writings of the previous century. And the poison was
drawn from the argument because it was a conflict within the
community of a University where teachers and taught were
held together by the bond of real community of respect and
affection.

But here was revolution, repudiation of the past, of
the doctrinaire bigotry of the age of Zeal, of the doctrine of
Predestination, and the return to the theme of Christianity as
a divine life. [28] These views were put forward with deep
learning and in prose of wonder: Peter Sterry and Nathaniel
Culverwell are in prose what Henry Purcell was in music.
Ralph Cudworth was a perfectionist who died with his best
work still in manuscript and Wesley rightly included his noble
oration to the House of Commons, March 31st 1647 on "The
Life of Christ, the Pith and Kernel of All Religion" with its
attack on

> our bookish Christians ... [who write] ... as if re-
> ligion were nothing but a little book craft, a mere
> paper skill.... But he is a true Christian indeed,
> not only that is book-taught, but that is God-taught
> ..., he that hath the Spirit of Christ within him
> .... Ink and paper can never make us Christians,
> can never beget a new nature in us, can never
> form Christ. [29]

If you read Heinrich Bornkamm's two sensitive essays
on Jacob Böhme you will understand why his writings had for
men like Henry More, John Byrom and William Law the kind

of attraction that Teilhard de Chardin has had in our day.[30]
But if you turn to Böhme's writings you will understand why
they shocked and horrified John Wesley as going dangerously
beyond the bounds of scripture, and that he understood the
menace of this kind of theosophy upon the more cultivated followers of the Revival.[31]

And then, a preoccupation with Predestination:

> We have no warrant in Scripture, to peep into those
> hidden rolls of eternity ... to persuade ourselves
> that we are elected to everlasting happiness; before
> we see the image of God, in righteousness and true
> holiness shared in our hearts.[32]

Not for nothing did Wesley conclude his sermon on "Reason"
by quoting the great Platonist text "The Spirit of Man is the
Candle of the Lord."[33]

But there is another facet of the Platonists to which
latterly Francis Yates and D. P. Walker have drawn attention.[34] They returned to Plato via the great Florentine Platonists of the 16th century, to Ficino and Mirandola and
through them to the Orphic mysteries, the Hermetic writings,
the Cabbals--edging on to a world of gnosticism, of white
magic and of alchemy. And not only the Platonists but the
new men of the Royal Society like Boyle and Isaac Newton had
not disentangled their science from a mystic theosophy which
was attractive but partly bogus, the kind of ferment surrounding the mysterious Rosicrucians, and the speculative mysticism of Paracelsus, Weigel and Jacob Böhme.[35] Yet Wesley
came to the very edge, within a hair's breadth of William
Law whom he never ceased to acclaim as a good and great
man and whose major treatises he himself published in later
years. Indeed, it is astonishing to discover how much John
Wesley had in common with men like Henry More and William

Law and John Byrom. There were moments in his life when
he might easily have become such as they were, what Belloc
called "remote and ineffectual dons," reading and meditating
and even retiring from the hubbub of life in a college, as
More did to Ragley and Law to Putney and Kingscliffe.

But John Wesley's story is not in the end about books
and ideas.   Henri Talon has finely said, "Books do not copy
books, but souls copy souls." The clash of ideas for him
came within the moving context of the great Revival.   The
differences between the evangelical Calvinists and Wesley's
evangelical Arminianism were not at first very important,
though they became so towards the end of his life, when Wesley was attacked with great bitterness by the Calvinists, who
gradually withdrew from his connection and from the link with
his itinerancy.

Wesley claimed to regard this as a difference of opinion (and could therefore refrain from speaking about it when
he went to Scotland), though he was hard put to it to justify
the expulsion of John Cennick and his friends if that were so.
But this was a true perception, for Arminianism and Calvinism, like Catholicism and Jansenism, were within a common
17th-century crisis of Augustinianism about the character, not
the existence, of grace.   It cannot be said that Whitefield's
Calvinism made him a more effective or less effective evangelist than Wesley--and vice versa.   A few years ago I bor-
rowed a distinction from the Catholic theologian Rondet and
suggested that Evangelical Arminianism, with its joyful universal offer of salvation--"For all, for all my Saviour died"--
represented an "optimism of grace" as against the "pessimism
of grace" which limited salvation to a few elect souls. [36]

But I have to admit that when Wesley included Henry
Scougal, the Scottish Episcopalian, in the Christian Library,

it was not his beautiful little "Life of God in the Soul of
Man" but sermons which include a terrible exposition of the
theme "That there are but a small number saved" which ends
with an attack on those who

> cannot imagine that heaven is such an empty and
> desolate place and have so few to inhabit it. [37]

Nor can we make too much of the difference between an Arminian and Calvinist view of the freedom of the human will.
We need to remember the profound comment of Berdyaev,
that it was the Calvinists who taught the bondage of the will,
who became the creators of human liberties, and the Jesuits,
with their insistence on freedom, who supported despotism.

Yet Scott Lidgett believed that there was a cheerfulness about the Arminian piety of his home and forebears
which was not so evident among the Calvinists.   And certainly for Alexander Knox this was a grand trait of John Wesley:

> His countenance, as well as conversation, expressed
> an habitual gaiety of heart, which nothing but con-
> scious virtue and innocence could have bestowed.
> He was, in truth, the most perfect specimen of
> moral happiness which I ever saw. [38]

Yet not for nothing did the "imitation of Christ" link the pattern of Methodism with the lay spirituality of the later Middle
Ages, with an austere life style which was a deliberate challenge to the extravagence and selfishness of the surrounding
world.   Plainness of speech, simplicity of dress--and he set
the example even if he had to spoil the opening of City Road
Chapel with a tirade against the elephantine bonnets in the
surrounding pews.   And of course, he may have known in his
heart that his own white hair, and the simple black fustian
which he wore so neatly made him a more comely figure
than any silks and powdered wigs.

But what converted men and women needed were not
ideas, or principles, or a bundle or synthesis of them called
Evangelical Arminianism, but Christ,

> Q. What sermons do we find, by experience to be
>   attended by the greatest blessing?
>
> A. Such as are most close, convincing, searching,
>   such as have most of Christ ... the most effec-
>   tual way of preaching Christ is to preach him
>   in all his offices and to declare His Law as well
>   as His gospel, both to believers and unbeliev-
>   ers. [39]

I remember a service at Littlemore, near Oxford,
commemorating John Henry Newman. A great French Catholic
was groping for a word with which to summarize Newman's
religion--"If we had to have a word for it," he said "we
might call it Scriptural Holiness." Well, there is room within the Bible for many patterns of godliness, but this was
where Wesley found his religion, in the combination of the
doctrines of justification by faith in Romans and Galatians
with the simple audacities of his beloved First Epistle of
John which led him to dare to take the Collect for Purity as
meaning what it says and God as willing to fulfill here and
now his promises of sanctifying grace. He did not think of
holiness as some 19th and 20th century movements have tended to do, as a kind of vague Scotch Mist, but with the or-
dered colors of an English garden, flowers and fruits of the
spirit, each with a color and a habitat and a name. "Our
doctrines" and "Our discipline" and "Our hymns" and "Our
literature" became a great frame of--to use a word despised
in our time--edification, of building up a people in grace.

His genius was for adaptation and improvisation. Like
Topsy, his Methodism "just growed."

> He was totally incapable [says Alexander Knox] of
> preconceiving such a scheme. This would have im-
> plied an exercise of forethought and politic contriv-
> ance, than which nothing could be more opposite to
> his whole mental constitution.... That he had un-
> common acuteness in fitting expedients to conjunc-
> tures is most certain; this, in fact, was his great
> talent. [40]

And so all the characteristic institutions of Methodism, the
class meeting, lay preachers, the itinerancy, the Conference,
were inspired improvisations. "Methodism came down out of
heaven," cried one too exuberant preacher, "as it was wanted, piece by piece."

    Like the multiplication of a simple life cell, the pat-
tern grew swiftly and ever more complex.

> I said, 'If all of you will meet on Thursday evening,
> I will advise you as well as I can.' The first eve-
> ning about twelve persons came: the next week,
> thirty or forty. When they were increased to a
> hundred I took down their names and places of
> abode. Thus without any plan or design [said Wes-
> ley] began the Methodist society in England.

Or, as he put it elsewhere, "two young clergymen" began to
travel, "hither and thither"[41] from London to Bristol and
then to Newcastle and then to a thousand towns and villages
between and across the border to Scotland and over the sea
to Ireland and the Norman Isles, and then beyond the Atlantic
and to Africa and the Pacific and the Islands of the seas."

    Wesley's England was a green and pleasant land to an
extent we can no longer conceive: the most lovely succession of open air theatres in Christian history, the cliffs of
Cornwall, the green bocage of Devon, the skies of East Ang-
lis, the swelling hills of Cumberland, the mountains of
Wales, the moors and valleys of the north and west, the
smooth backs of the Downs.

And as he preached in Cornwall in the Gwennap pit,
with his back to the last rays of a setting sun, in the quiet
of an English summer evening, where not a breath, not a
leaf, not one of thousands of human beings stirred, and all
melted into one in the growing darkness as they hung on the
words of one who commended his Saviour--how right he was,
how much more solemn and beautiful and majestic the scene
which God had wrought than any Gothic imitation, how much
less marvelous the acoustics of the new preaching boxes in
Norwich or on City Road, London.

> Ye mountains and vales in praises abound
> Ye hills and ye dales continue the sound
> Break forth into singing, ye trees of the wood
> For Jesus is bringing lost sinners to God.

Of course, sometimes in England it rains. And so
he came to the front of the curtains of wind and rain and
storm, and often snow so deep that his congregations melted
down to two or three, but he continued his pilgrim's progress. "One here will valiant be, come wind, come weather."

And the towns: Christopher Wren's new churches, and
the even newer fostering mushroom slums--and Bristol and
Oxford and even Manchester, walled around with gardens and
babbling of green fields. And the people--the tinners of Cornwall, the keelmen of Newcastle, the colliers of Kingswood and
Staffordshire, the drunkards, swearers, sabbath breakers at
Moorfields and the harlots of Drury Lane. And the mobs
which he turned into companies of devout, decent people
clothed and in their right minds, sitting at the feet of Jesus,
changing the morals and manners of whole communities. Not
a scene to be romanticized, for it was an age of great cruel-
ty and callousness and need, such that unimaginable horrors
must have befallen the nation in the Industrial Revolution with-

out the revival of decencies and compassion.   There is a
terrible passage in one of Wesley's sermons:

> That the people suffer, none can deny.... Thou-
> sands of people in the West of England, throughout
> Cornwall in particular, in the north and even in
> the midland counties, are totally unemployed....
> I have seen not a few of these wretched creatures
> ... standing in the streets, with pale looks, hol-
> low eyes, and meagre limbs; or creeping up and
> down like walking shadows.   I have known families,
> who a few years ago lived in an easy, genteel
> manner, reduced to just as much raiment as they
> had on, and as much food as they could gather in
> a field.   To this one or other of them repaired
> once a day to pick up the turnips which the cattle
> had left; which they boiled, if they could get a few
> sticks, or otherwise ate them raw. [42]

He spent thousands of hours in what his diary calls
"conversation: tea"--which is, I suppose, a true prognosti-
cation of a British Methodism which surely deserves to have
a cup of tea rampant emblazoned on its arms.   And the thousands of men and women who opened their homes and fed
and boarded the preachers on their rounds, a wonderful tradition of Christian friendship and hospitality which has never
died.   And his young men and his old helpers--from the Per-
ronets and Gambold at one end to Coke and Fletcher of Mad-
eley at the other, from John Nelson to Adam Clarke, not officer class but officer material, like Nelson's captains a
band of brothers and, like Napoleon's Marshals, dedicated
warriors.

And then his ladies.   In 1959 Dr. Lofthouse wrote
two fine articles in Wesley's Chapel Magazine about them. [43]

> It is certain [said Alexander Knox] that Mr. Wesley
> had a predilection for the female character ...
> finding in females a quicker and fuller responsive-
> ness to his own ideas of interior piety and affec-
> tionate devotion. [44]

Nothing strange about this, for it was in the tradition of John Bradford and John Knox, and St. Francis of Sales and Fenelon. Not only because, as Jean Guitton has said, writing to ladies lessens the pain of writing letters. But it was a score of these, Mary Bishop and Hannah Ball, and Mary Bosanquet, who understood and used the Christian Library as devout women had best understood St. Bernard and Meister Eckhart and John Tauler in other centuries in that succession of a ministry of women which goes back to Galilee and for which Protestantism has taken too little heed and thought. And not individuals but bands, classes, societies, devout companies.

Having in recent days reread all the Journals and all the Letters from beginning to end, I cannot but say a word about the Old Wesley. Certainly we cannot drive a wedge between the Old Wesley and The Young, and the continuities are plain to see.

> I cannot write a better sermon on the Good Steward than I could seven years ago [he wrote in 1778]; I cannot write a better sermon on the Great Assize than I did twenty years ago; I cannot write a better on The Use of Money than I did nearly thirty years ago; nay, I know not that I could write a better on the Circumcision of the Heart than I did five-and-forty years ago.... Forty years ago I knew and preached every Christian doctrine which I preach now. [45]

And if occasionally he was querulous and demanding and autocratic, there is the wonderfully appealing picture of a good, kind, holy and affectionate old man, breathing the love of God and of his fellow men. In those last years he had become a respected national figure, whom William Wilberforce and John Howard sought out, and whom old General Oglethorpe in his eighties stopped to kiss his hand.

We see him, in his eighties, bare-headed on four bitter

winter mornings, begging from door to door, his feet always immersed in the melting snow, and not resting until he had two hundred pounds with which to feed and clothe his poor.

And then his last visit to Cornwall, to the town of Falmouth:

> The last time I was here was above forty years ago [at 86 he had forgotten he had been there twice since]. I was there taken prisoner by an immense mob, gaping and roaring like lions. But how is the tide turned! High and low now lined the street, from one end of the town to the other, out of stark love and kindness, gaping and staring as if the King were going by.[46]

No, not a King, but assuredly a great ambassador. A man worth queueing up and waiting hours just to see, a man worth remembering, this apostle of England.

NOTES

1. "Anglican" is a 19th-century term and to a surprising extent conditions discussion in terms of hindsight, in terms of 19th-century parties--Anglo Catholic, Evangelical and Broad Church. The result is such a biased and one-sided if splendid anthology as that of Cross and More's "Anglicanism" and some descriptions of an Anglican "Via Media" which make very disputable reading of the 17th century, not least in the place of Richard Hooker who in no way dominated Church of England divinity in the 17th and 18th centuries.

2. Sermon "On Zeal," in The Works of the Rev. John Wesley [edited by Thomas Jackson] (London: Wesleyan Conference Office, 1872), Vol. VII, p. 54.

3. Ibid., p. 64.

4. I find the 18th-century phrase, "inward religion," best to use. The word "spirituality" has Catholic undertones and the phrase fits the catholicity of Wesley's Christian Library and solves as much as anything can

the question of the relation of mysticism to devotion.

5. No doubt in John Worthington's edition of 1677 which in-
    troduced the title which John Wesley kept, "The Chris-
    tian's Pattern."

6. Samuel Wesley, "Advice to a Young Clergyman," re-
    printed as an appendix in Thomas Jackson's The Life
    of the Rev. Charles Wesley (London: John Mason,
    1841), Vol. II, pp. 500-534.

7. Ibid., p. 510.

8. Ibid., pp. 521-522.

9. Ibid., p. 524ff.

10. Works, X, pp. 480-500.

11. Works, X, p. 483.

12. "An Address to the Clergy," 1756, Works, X, pp. 483,
    491-492.

13. Letters, edited by Telford, V, p. 110.

14. Journal, March 23, 1749, edited by Curnock, III, p.
    391.

15. Journal, June 16, 1788, edited by Curnock, VII, pp.
    352-353.

16. "A Compendium of Logic," Works, XIV, p. 189.

17. G. E. M. Anscombe, Introduction to Wittgenstein's Trac-
    tatus, 4th ed. (London: Hutchinson, 1971).

18. "Preface to Sermons on Several Occasions," 1788,
    Works, VI, pp. 186-187.

19. Journal, June 5, 1766, edited by Curnock, V, p. 169.

20. Sermon, "The Wisdom of God's Counsels," Works, VI,
    p. 328.

21. Journal, Sept. 20, 1759, ed. Curnock, IV, p. 354.

22.   Norman Sykes, Church and State in England in the 18th
      Century (London: University Press, 1934), p. 398.

23.   Sermon, "The Case of Reason Impartially Considered,"
      in Works, VI, p. 359f.

24.   Alexander Knox, "Remarks on the Life and Character
      of John Wesley," in Robert Southey, Life of Wesley,
      edited by Maurice H. Fitzgerald (London: Oxford
      University Press, 1925), vol. II, pp. 352-353, 357.

25.   "Minutes of the Conference, 1744-1745," in Publications
      of the Wesley Historical Society, No. 1 (London: Wes-
      ley Historical Society, 1896), pp. 10, 22.

26.   Letters, ed. Telford, IV, p. 122.

27.   Alexander Knox, "Remarks on the Life and Character
      of John Wesley," in Robert Southey, Life of Wesley,
      edited by Maurice H. Fitzgerald (London: Oxford Uni-
      versity Press, 1925), Vol. II, p. 345.

28.   It also made Cambridge open to a new scientific age,
      as the great Botanist John Ray attested.

29.   Ralph Cudworth, "The Life of Christ, the Pith and Ker-
      nel of All Religion; a Sermon preached before the
      Honourable House of Commons at Westminster, March
      31, 1647," in Wesley's Christian Library (London:
      T. Blanshard, 1820), Vol. IX, pp. 376-377.

30.   Heinrich Bornkamm, "Jakob Böhme, Leben und Wirkung"
      and "Jakob Böhme, der Denker" in his Das Jahrhund-
      ert der Reformation, Gestalten und Kräfte, Zweite,
      Vermehrte Auflage (Göttingen: Vandenhoeck & Rup-
      recht, 1966), pp. 315-331, 331-345.   On William Law
      and John Wesley see John Brazier Green's John Wes-
      ley and William Law (London: Epworth, 1945), Eric
      W. Baker's A Herald of the Evangelical Revival: A
      Critical Inquiry into the Relationship of William Law
      to John Wesley and the Beginnings of Methodism
      (London: Epworth, 1948) and A. Keith Walker's
      William Law, His Life and Thought (London: SPCK,
      1973).

31.   For Wesley's comments on Boehme, see his "Thoughts
      Upon Jacob Behmen," 1780 in his Works, IX, pp. 509-

518 and his Journal, IV, p. 409 and especially III, p.
17: "I met once with the works of a celebrated author, of whom many great men cannot speak without
rapture and the strongest expressions of admiration--
I mean Jacob Behmen.... What can I say? ... it
is most sublime nonsense, inimitable bombast, fustian not to be parelleled!"
  For Wesley's comments on Law see his "Extract of
a Letter to the Reverend Mr. Law occasioned by some
of his late writings, 1756," Works, IX, pp. 466-509.
See also The Private Journal and Literary Remains
of John Byrom, edited by Richard Parkinson (Manchester: Printed for the Chetham Society, 1854-57),
pt. 2, Vol. II for the statement that Wesley read out
a group of Boehmist and William Law addicts from
his society.

32. Ralph Cudworth, "The Life of Christ the Pith and Ker-
     nel of All Religion; a Sermon preached before the
     Honourable House of Commons at Westminster, March
     31, 1647," in Wesley's Christian Library (London:
     T. Blanshard, 1820), vol. IX, pp. 378-379.

33. Sermon, "The Case of Reason Impartially Considered,"
     Works, VI, p. 351.

34. Frances A. Yates, Giordano Bruno and the Hermetic
     Tradition (Chicago: University of Chicago Press,
     1964) and her The Rosicrucian Enlightenment (London:
     Routledge and Kegan Paul, 1974); Daniel P. Walker,
     The Ancient Theology: Studies in Christian Platonism
     from the 15th to the 18th Century (Ithaca, N. Y.:
     Cornell University Press, 1972); Charles E. Trink-
     haus, In Our Image and Likeness: Humanity and Di-
     vinity in Italian Humanist Thought (Chicago: Univer-
     sity of Chicago Press, 1970), 2 vols.

35. Heinrich Bornkamm, Das Jahrhundert der Reformation,
     2., verm. Aufl. (Göttingen: Vandenhoeck und Rup-
     recht, 1966); Alexandre Koyré, Mystiques, Spirituels,
     Alchemistes: Schwenckfeld, Seb. Franck, Weigel,
     Paracelse, (Paris: A. Colin, 1955); Serge Hutin,
     Les Disciples Anglais de Jacob Boehme Aux XVIIe et
     XVIIIe Siècles (Paris: Éditions Denoël, 1960).

36. Gordon Rupp, Methodism in Relation to Protestant Tra-
     dition (London: Epworth Press, 1954), p. 20. The

"Optimism of Grace," as I use the term, must be
distinguished from the optimism of the Enlightenment.
According to Peter Gay, the word appears in mid-
18th century just in time to be shattered by the Lisbon
earthquake!

37.   Henry Scougal, "Discourses on Important Subjects," in
      Wesley's Christian Library (London: J. Kershaw,
      1825), Vol. 23, p. 413.

38.   Alexander Knox, "Remarks on the life and character of
      John Wesley," in Robert Southey, Life of Wesley, ed-
      ited by Maurice H. Fitzgerald (London: Oxford Uni-
      versity Press, 1925), vol. II, p. 344.

39.   "Minutes of the Conference, May 14, 1746, in Minutes
      of the Methodist Conferences from the First Held in
      London by the Late Rev. John Wesley in the Year
      1744 (London: John Mason, 1862), Vol. I, p. 32.

40.   Alexander Knox, "Remarks on the life and character of
      John Wesley," in Robert Southey, Life of Wesley, ed-
      ited by Maurice H. Fitzgerald (London: Oxford Univer-
      sity Press, 1925), vol. II, p. 353.

41.   Sermon, "On God's Vineyard," 1787, Works, VII, pp.
      206-207.

42.   Sermon, "National Sins and Miseries" 1775, Works,
      VII, p. 402.

43.   W. F. Lofthouse, "Wesley and his women correspondents,"
      Wesley's Chapel Magazine, January and April, 1959,
      pp. [2-8], [6-12].

44.   Alexander Knox, "Remarks on the life and character of
      John Wesley," in Robert Southey, Life of Wesley, ed-
      ited by Maurice H. Fitzgerald (London: Oxford Univer-
      sity Press, 1925), vol. II, p. 339.

45.   Journal, Sept. 1, 1778, ed. Curnock, VI, p. 209.

46.   Journal, August 18, 1789, ed. Curnock, VIII, p. 3.

CHAPTER III

WESLEY'S PLACE IN CHURCH HISTORY

Martin Schmidt

When we want to determine the place of a man and a movement in church history we need first of all to raise and settle the question about the relationship between the man and the movement. Was John Wesley the exponent of a movement, or did he in reverse create and direct a movement?

The movement which preceded his appearance has been justly called "the religious societies within the Church of England." During the reign of Charles II, the monarch who had spent his years of exile in France (1646ff) in close connection with the court of Versailles, and who had brought with him lasting impressions of the luxurious and licentious life there, young people of the higher society in London felt deeply dissatisfied with the voluptuousness and dissipation which they saw and experienced every day. Life seemed to them meaningless. Uneasiness of mind and discomfort on various levels led to several suicides. Looking for consolation and guidance they found Anthony Horneck (1641-1697), pastor of the Savoy Church to be the right man.

Horneck was a native of Bacharach in the German Rhineland, of Protestant parentage and a subject of the Elec-

tor Palatine.   After a good theological training both at Heidelberg and Leiden Universities he emigrated to Britain about
1661, studied at Queen's College, Oxford and joined the Church
of England.   He was no outspoken Calvinist.   The only feeble
token pointing in that direction was an early prize won in the
field of Old Testament studies for a dissertation on Jeph-
thah's sacrifice of his daughter.   The gifted young church historian Johann Heinrich Hottinger (1620-1667), who left Heidelberg after a few years, returning to his home city Zurich,
gave Horneck an extradorinarily high commendation in a recently discovered testimony in Latin which Hottinger had
carelessly taken with him to Zurich, where it is preserved
in the archives of the Central Library.   It is possible that
Horneck adhered, during his days on the Continent, to the
new Pietism then developing in Holland and in the adjacent
Rhinelands.   In England he adjusted himself completely to the
mainstream Anglican Patristic and devotional mind.   When
his library, an unusually rich collection, had to be sold after his death, it contained many works of the Greek and Latin Fathers of the early Church, but not a single German or
Dutch book was listed.   His own publications consisted mainly, if not exclusively, of devotional manuals, such as The
Happy Ascetick (1681), The Fire of the Altar (1683) and The
Crucified Jesus (1686), which Wesley extracted and published
in his Christian Library (vol. 28).   Horneck was apparently
a pious man, with a special gift for pastoral care which he
proved once in an extremely difficult case.   Now, in 1678,
the young gentlemen and ladies approached him.   He helped
them by forming small groups for Bible-reading, self-exam-
ination, and mutual pastoral care by exchanging their experiences and speaking frankly.

The youngsters, whom he formed into small groups,

did not limit themselves to introversion.   After a while, we cannot precisely state when, they wanted, as young people are normally inclined to, to achieve some solid and visible work for others.   They started social work of all sorts-- visiting prisoners, aiding poor families, establishing scholar- ships for the illiterate poor in charity schools, publishing and distributing Bibles and devotional tracts like the famous Puritan devotional, The Whole Duty of Man (1659), among the lower classes of the population--in order to promote Christianity in an age of indifference and irreligion.   It could easily be seen that such activities proved an excellent instru- ment for awakening dull parishes.   And we ought not be sur- prised to learn from the archives of the permanent establish- ment of the Society for Promoting Christian Knowledge in London in 1698, and that John Wesley's father Samuel (1666- 1735) at Epworth hailed the movement and helped found a lo- cal branch.   John Wesley was, no doubt, from his early days acquainted with the atmosphere and purpose of this movement. Thus, when in 1735 he accepted the call of the SPCK to go as a missionary to Georgia in America, extended to him by Dr. John Burton, he entered into a well-known movement.

For out of this Religion Society movement inaugurated by Anthony Horneck and chronicled by Josiah Woodward origi- nated the two important societies already mentioned--SPCK, today the main publishing house of the Church of England, and the SPG (Society for the Propagation of the Gospel in Foreign Parts, founded 1701), which New England's Cotton Mather ironically labeled: "The Society for the Molestation of the Gospel in Foreign Parts."   These two organizations were im- portant also since contact was immediately made with them by Augustus Hermann Francke (1663-1727) and his orphanage at Halle, the center of Pietism in Central Europe with ecumenical aspirations.

Thus the ground was very well prepared for the appearance of Methodism and Wesley's plan for it as a religious society in and for the Church of England. All the requirements existed. The religious society movement in England had come to a considerable prosperity when Wesley reached maturity. Could he bring it to full flower?

Characteristic features link Wesley's Methodism and England's Religious Society tradition: first, the concern for pastoral care, for personal religion, the endeavor to do good as much as possible, the intention to convert dull Christians into living members of the Body of Christ, the concern for education, the commitment to foreign missions; finally, the devotional and Biblical orientation. All this, however, is not sufficient for making Wesley the exponent and developer of such aims and tendencies. For there are obvious differences between both movements as well.

First, Biblical adherence is for Wesley really fundamental. It is not just one element beside others, but the very substance and character based on an outspoken indebtedness to early Christianity. Even his language and his literary style were largely shaped by elements of the Greek New Testament and the early Christian writings. Moreover, the proclamation of the Gospel in preaching was for Wesley essential. It could never be replaced or substituted by distributing tracts or a program of Christian education. He regarded the offering of the good news from God to all mankind wherever he reached them as his bounden duty, and his legal right as a fellow of Lincoln College, Oxford to preach across the land as providentially instrumental. In addition, the element of theological reasoning and argument, for instance on original sin, belonged for him to the gist of the Christian life and ex-

istence. So, in spite of the different heritages--Anglican,
Puritan, Continental Pietism and the native British Religious
Society tradition--Wesley printed his own unique stamp on
Methodism and gave special characteristic features to its
complexion. And I want to add something which was for me
also an important enrichment. He never showed a condes-
cending attitude in dealing with plain folk, as perhaps leaders
of other religious societies might have shown. So I feel we
are correct in regarding Wesley from the historical point of
view as an independent figure in the bias and in the core of
his theological and ecclesiastical significance.

Second, in all great men in church history, we discover a coincidence of intense personal religion, a commitment to their task and mission, devotion to theological reflection, and surprisingly, of decisive events occurring in the
course of their lives. As Dr. Outler has already pointed out,
it is too narrow to speak only of one conversion of Wesley in
1738 at Aldersgate. We have to see his life as a series of
conversions. That means that he was always open to new
possibilities and insights into the depth and variety of the
Christian message and mission. Therefore we find ourselves
compelled by the impact of crucial facts to describe and in-
terpret them on the lines of a theological biography, showing
the coincidence and concentration. From my point of view
Wesley, especially when compared to Zinzendorf, shows a
unique theological and Biblical concentration. There is nothing of this playing attitude which made Count Zinzendorf
charming for his time--not for everybody of course, and especially not for Wesley. But Zinzendorf was a figure who
was really in many ways an expression and a true embodiment
of the Baroque attitude of the 18th century. Wesley was
quite different from him both in manner and temperament.

After a short personal encounter Wesley was impressed, at
least for a while, but Zinzendorf and Wesley soon parted company.

Theology means for men like Wesley nothing theoretical or additional to their practice, not an over-structure. It
is, in fact, a true reflection of their personal experience, not
an attempt to systematize them. Professor Outler expressed
this in the best possible manner in his introduction to Wesley's writings in his volume in the Library of Protestant
Thought series:

> [Wesley] seems never to have felt the impulse to
> produce anything resembling a comprehensive exposi-
> tion of his theological ideas--and this may have been
> just as well. Short doctrinal summaries are scat-
> tered throughout his writings, and these give ample
> evidence that his thought was consciously organized
> around a stable core of basic coordinated motifs.
> But there is no extended development of his system,
> and for the simple reason that there never seemed
> to be a practical need for such a thing. His single,
> sufficient motive in theologizing was to reinforce the
> spiritual and ethical concerns of his societies in par-
> ticular and the Church in general. Theology, in
> this context, was a dialectical affair: faith seeking
> self-awareness and self-expression [and I would add
> myself self-assurance]. This neglect of a developed
> systematic statement, however, has encouraged all
> too many of his followers to misconceive the organ-
> ic unity of Wesley's thought, or to ignore the pivot-
> al place or rational understanding in his mind and
> method. Wesley himself cannot be invoked on be-
> half of an anti-intellectual attitude toward Christian
> truth. [1]

Third, Wesley's sermons, in spite of their immediate
appeal to the heart and to the will, reflect sound reasoning on
Biblical themes. One can clearly state and demonstrate where
his emphases lay: justification by faith as a personal experience of God's overwhelming grace, free grace; regeneration--

or better--"new birth" as a complete renewal of man with
Christian perfection as one's goal and prospect--perfection in
love as the incarnation of holiness in personal life combined
with happiness; the witness of the Holy Spirit in joy and
peace; the characteristic synthesis between a serious concern
for Sanctification, earnest discipline of an almost ascetical
sort, and cheerfulness in being saved from sin and the wrath
of God. All this may be briefly formulated in the equation:
Holiness Is Happiness. This equation has a considerable tradition in British theology, surprisingly both Anglican (dating
from Richard Hooker, ca. 1554-1600) and Puritan. I have
found ample evidence of this equation of holiness and happiness in both streams of British theology--even Anglo-Cathol-
icism and radical Puritanism. New birth is intended to reshape the original image of God implanted in man; or, as
Wesley usually puts it, according to Philippians 2:5, "Have
this mind among yourselves, which you have in Christ Jesus. "
All other subjects are subordinate to these--for instance,
humility, the dominant value in English religious and moral
thought, or Christian freedom from the law, or even the role
of law in Christian practice. The same is true for the doctrine of the Church and the Sacraments, though Wesley remained throughout his long life deeply attached to both church
and sacraments. He strenuously objected to an independent,
individualistic, non-church-related, non-sacramentally con-
firmed approach to the Christian life. Especially when he
treated the doctrine of the Church, he interpreted her as the
People of God called out of the world, united into one new
congregation and determined to become holy, to walk according to the precious vocation she had received.

This concentration helps to explain why "the people
called Methodists" under his guidance stood firm despite all

persecution and remained stubbornly loyal to the central
Christian truths. How deeply he was bound to the Scripture
himself can be seen in one of his late letters to an American
preacher, Freeborn Garrettson, which he wrote at the age of
almost 86. Here Wesley blames Garrettson for using the
phrase "finding freedom to do this or that." Wesley advised
him, or rather, commanded him thus:

> If I have plain Scripture or plain reason for doing
> a thing well, these are my rules, and my only
> rules. I regard not whether I had freedom or no.
> This is an unscriptural expression and a very fal-
> lacious rule. I wish to be in every point, great
> and small, a Scriptural, rational Christian. [2]

This may sound like a legalistic interpretation of
Scripture, as if the Bible were a collection of laws and commandments. But this would be a complete misinterpretation
of what Wesley had in mind. Holy Scripture was in his hands
a book of life, to be proved and applied by personal experience. He identified himself and his followers with the Biblical persons, with their situations and decisions, their habits
and their attitudes, their scruples and their deliverances. As
to the Commandments he did not use them in their Old Testament context. Rather he took them in the form our Lord
gave to them in his Sermon on the Mount. Wesley knew well
enough that the level of the Old Testament, with its almost
equal emphasis on cultic, ceremonial and moral commandments, had been superseded and overcome by Jesus Christ.
He did not even deal with such questions as St. Paul raises,
whether Christians should hold a law in regard to their weak-
er brethren, a law whose validity they were no longer convinced of. Due to the Antinomian troubles during the early
stage of the Methodist movement, brought to a head by Philip
Heinrich Molther (1714-1780), a Moravian from Alsace who

had apparently come under the influence of French quietistic mysticism, Wesley emphasized the equal importance of law and Gospel in Scripture. Molther's "German Stillness" must have seemed to Wesley a reiteration of William Law's mystical "nonsense" which he reacted so vehemently against after his conversion. He blamed Luther as well as Count Zinzendorf for their, as he assumed, complete rejection of the law. What Wesley tried to achieve was a balanced evaluation of both elements which he found in Scripture. And the all-exceeding, all-overshadowing authority of Christ prevailed so strongly upon him that he felt committed to follow Him in any respect. The Pauline reasoning on law and freedom, the argument on law in its coherence with death and ultimate damnation, the Pauline apprehension of falling back to the level of the Israelites--all this did not appeal to Wesley as a personal command of Jesus, his master and Lord. And here we perceive a kind of modern approach. The Bible is taken as a message as well as a personal commitment. Wesley's personal identification with Scripture is typical for the 18th century and the following centuries. Like modern interpreters Wesley did not regard Scripture as a mere book with certain contents, but as a testimony of a speaking Lord. So Wesley personalized Scripture. The personal adherence and loyalty to Christ, the personal appearance and presence of the Lord in the pages of Holy Scripture--these were the data, the categories which Wesley regarded as appropriate.

Of course, from the Lutheran theological standpoint Wesley's equal stress on law and Gospel seems a deviating position. For the German reformer, who no doubt followed Paul not only in his Epistles to the Romans and to the Galatians, but also in his letters to the Corinthians (especially II Corinthians 3) and to the Philippians (especially chapter 3),

the law contained in the Old Testament and given originally
to the Israelites is clearly subordinate to the Gospel which
announces full forgiveness of sin and opens the way for a new
existence as regenerate children of God starting a fresh life
without any burden of the former life.

On the other hand, from the angle of a church historian two questions are not settled. Perhaps they can never
be satisfactorily solved. Did Luther himself do full justice
to the commandments of Jesus in the Sermon on the Mount,
or was he, especially in his opposition to the morally-minded
Erasmus, prejudiced and therefore one-sided? Would John
Wesley have gotten the same impression of Antinominianism
if he had had not Molther and Zinzendorf as his opponents
but Luther himself?

Since I have been asked to examine the theme "Wesley's Place in the Christian Tradition" from a Lutheran
Perspective, I would state the following conclusions:

First, the approach to the Bible was different for Luther and Wesley. Luther, coming from the Middle Ages and
its dogmatic-ontological view, took the Scriptures more as a
dogmatic document than Wesley, who in the Age of Enlightenment used it as a personal testimony of the voice of Jesus
and the voices of the Apostles. There was certainly no difference between Luther and Wesley regarding the binding
character of the content of Scripture. But the approach was
different. The argument on theological propositions and their
logical coherence in the age of Wesley no longer had the
force, the compelling and convincing power, as in Luther's
time. Instead, the personal authority of Jesus as Lord and
Master of his followers had increased. The difference made
it possible not to delete or to reject Pauline arguments, but
to put them behind.

Secondly, Luther's background was the Roman Catholic Church of the late Middle Ages. That means a church deeply, perhaps substantially, structured on juridical lines. The church as the Body of Christ appeared as a universal collective entity, bound together by the sacramental unity, divided into sacramental channels as well as directed by commandments, by juridical orders and regulations. A kind of sacramental rite, of sacramental jurisdiction, marshalled the whole life of Christians. Law was everywhere present and virulent.

For Wesley an equivalent of that situation did not exist. Therefore the problem of law and legalism did not so much affect him as Luther, who in addition found around him a new legalistic understanding of the Christian life in the Anabaptist stream. Perhaps, oversimplifying, one could say Wesley's age was menaced by the opposite extreme--the secular celebration of freedom and the growing indifference to Christian values, the law as well as the Gospel--while Luther's age had to fight against the confusion of law and Gospel in Christianity which ended up in a complete legalistic distortion of the Christian message to the world. If my judgment is correct, we do not have to choose between Luther and Wesley. Rather we are entitled to respect and accept both theologians. As to the practical character of their theology, I see no difference at all.

Thirdly, both Luther and Wesley use their theological reasoning not for mere speculation but for reinforcing the principal Christian truths. Their theology appears in close connection with their normal responsibility for carrying out the Christian message to their generation. Even when Luther seems to speculate in the controversies with Zwingli on the Eucharist and with Erasmus on the freedom of the will, he

attempts to maintain and to elucidate the Biblical truth, when
forced to speculation by the opponent and his argument, with
all the instrumentality of the Aristotelian tradition.

Fourthly, coming back to the law and Gospel, I suggest we pay attention to Wesley's remark in the days of his
conversion, that he looked upon the Bible as one great promise from beginning to end.   I am also convinced that Wesley
held a meaningful hermeneutic, meaningful even in our overly
intellectualized century today. [3]   Wesley's stress on the Bible
as promise shows a deep spiritual kinship and similarity to
Luther.

Fifthly, in spite of the principal similarity, there remains a difference between Luther and Wesley.   For Wesley,
the starting point was the aim of recovering Primitive Christianity, wherefore he was even nicknamed so.   Primitive
Christianity became a slogan in early 18th century England.
John Jewell's 1562 Apologia Ecclesiae Anglicanae delineated
the Patristic tradition of the Church of England in the Eliza-
bethan era.   It was also the slogan of the humanistic and
Arian reformers who wished to reshape orthodox Christian
doctrine in accordance with Enlightenment themes.   William
Whiston (1667-1752), originally a friend of the religious societies and even a member of the SPCK, wrote from 1709
onwards a four-volume work on Primitive Christianity Revived in which he intended to introduce Arianism and Socinian-
ism into the Church of England.   Whiston was deeply convinced that they represented genuine primitive Christianity.   It
was a serious attempt, though abortive, competing with the classical Anglican concept of patristic thought and practice as the
Christian norm.   Wesley shared the classical Anglican tradition of the restitution of early Christianity, not, I would say,
as an institution or organization, but as a personal experi-

ence. During his intense study of early Christianity represented by the New Testament, he insisted on reading and
quoting the New Testament in its original Greek. He discovered gradually that the center, the heart of Primitive Christianity, was justification by faith and sanctification--perfec-
tion in love. He identified himself with the men of the New
Testament, with the original disciples of Jesus Christ, while
for Luther the objective message of the New Testament remained primary. Here I see a real difference which is partly a difference of ages, but also a difference of personal ap-
proaches.

Sixthly, the high valuation of personal experience, of
personal encounter, of the exchange of personal experiences,
appears almost unique in Wesley. This brings him close to
the early Christians if we take the Pauline and other Epistles
of the New Testament in their original setting as testimonies
of personal, private, experiential piety--which they are, at
least in part. But Wesley's position also has affinities to
modern times, when the authority of written documents, of
tradition, and of institutions, no longer count as much as
personal experience.

This weight of personal experience as a determining
factor is new in church history. It appears on several levels and in different relationships during Wesley's life. First
of all, it becomes visible in the early exchange of impressions, feelings, judgments, thoughts and reflections with his
extraordinary mother, and even if not documented, with his
father. I'm convinced we must take more seriously Samuel's
influence on his son. Later, we see it in his close relationship with his friends and his brother at Oxford in the Holy
Club. Still later it is apparent in his encounter with the
two groups of German pietism--the Herrnhut Moravians and

two young Halle-trained pastors, Johann Martin Bolzius and
Israel Christian Gronau of the Salzburger settlement at New
Ebenezer in Georgia.   It shapes his conversations with
August Spangenberg, Peter Böhler, and Count Zinzendorf and
affects his theological method.   Wesley's high valuation of
personal experience reaches its climax in his lifelong correspondence with his lay preachers and with the male and fe-
male members of the Methodist Societies.

Further, we must never forget the importance of biog-
raphies for his personal use, as well as their recommenda-
tion by him to his correspondents through the years.   High
on Wesley's list were the accounts of the pious lives of Gas-
ton Jean Baptiste de Renty (1611-1649), a young French
nobleman from Normandy; Gregory Lopez (1542-1596), a hermit in Madrid and Mexico during the 16th century; and the
Scottish theologian and professor at St. Andrews, Thomas
Haylburton (1674-1712).   The life of de Renty ranked first in
Wesley's mind.   Wesley regarded de Renty, like his biogra-
pher Pierre Poiret, as the real Christian par excellence.   It
is very interesting to note that Wesley compared Count Zinzendorf, when he met him, to this model saint.   Of course,
Zinzendorf failed to measure up to this model.   De Renty,
who reached only the age of 38 years, was devotionally a pu-
pil of Pierre de Bérulle (1575-1629), the French Cardinal,
theologian and reformer who re-established the Italian Oratory
of Holy Love.   His life in the continual presence of God made
de Renty independent of the sacramental channels of the Roman Church.   He felt the presence of the Holy Trinity immediately in his own soul.   He dedicated his personal life, his
fortune, and his position in society completely to the service
of God, separating himself from his family, though only tem-
porarily and without any estrangement.   He gave himself to

the care of sick people, especially to those who suffered from ugly, repulsive and distasteful diseases, doing himself the most humiliating services, completely disregarding the danger of contagion. He went to the artisans, into their workshops, and founded the first Christian trade unions, not in order to enhance any leadership ambitions he may have had, but to build up common responsibility and common endeavor in the service of persons in need. For Wesley, de Renty obviously had reached what he had in mind when he spoke of Christian perfection in love. De Renty was no monk, no hermit, no ascetic. He lived in the world but without pretention, as St. Paul called upon the Corinthians to live as those who have this world's goods and give them away without pain and sorrow and to perform genuine Christian liberty (I Corinthians 7:29-31). Christians were free to use God's gifts, as an instrument for doing good to others without the least Pharisaic claim to merit in the eyes of God.

For Wesley it was crucial to follow this Biblical pattern of the Christian life. Wesley's sense of reality, or we should say his hunger for reality, was satisfied by reports of this kind. Therefore it meant much to him that the plain Moravian brethren of Hernnhut, especially Christian David (1691-1751) and Arvid Gradin the Swede,[4] told him their life stories, concealing nothing of their experiences, laying bare their hopes and failures, as Wesley himself had done with unlimited plainness and honesty in his own journal. Wesley was often deeply moved and sometimes influenced by the experiences of others. He did not always depend on his own impressions and thus did not limit the field to his own personal experience. The high valuation of experience is one of the typical features and characteristic peculiarities of modern church history. Its roots can be found in the development of

mysticism at the end of the Middle Ages. However, the new
authority of experience as verification of Scriptural values
and dogmatic assertions did not really become prevalent before the 18th century, when French quietistic mysticsm,
German pietism, and English Methodism all moved in the
same direction. It is part of Wesley's place in church history that he contributed in so influential and representative
a manner to this development.

Seventhly, throughout his long life Wesley emphasized
the common life of Christians. His experiences while a student at Oxford in the Holy Club, a band of serious students
who studied the New Testament in the original Greek and attempted to practice doing good to every person, reviving the
pattern of the Religious Societies, satisfied Wesley so deeply
that he refused to become his father's assistant and successor as a parish priest. He was convinced that his own holiness depended on the holiness of his fellows; therefore he
could not leave Oxford. The only reason he accepted the
call to Georgia lay in the fact that he would be accompanied
by three of his closest friends. The common life in the
Body of Christ--to use Fr. Lionel Thornton's famous modern
title[5]--was to Wesley the fundamental condition of his existence. This conviction did not exclude dictatorship in the
Methodist movement: Wesley was convinced that a strong
leader was required in order to maintain this common life.
Perhaps he overestimated his own position as indispensable
within his movement, as it frequently happens in history.
Seen from a Lutheran angle, I am inclined to excuse him for
that. For Luther at various times and occasions expressed
his view that he was only a mean tool, a very tiny tool, in
God's own hands; that Melanchthon was in many ways more
gifted than he, and that God could raise up many men like

himself (multos Martinos).   But when he was actually taken
away and Melanchthon had to take over responsibility for the
movement, everything went in the wrong direction.   The
Zwickau prophets invaded Wittenberg during Luther's stay at
Wartburg, and a disastrous theological disorientation and un-
certainty occurred in Lutheranism after Luther's death in
1546.

Wesley was a modern man, equipped with a sense of
organization, perhaps even a sense of management of affairs,
including financial resources.   He upheld an authoritarian
system during his lifetime and recommended an aristocratic
system in democratic form after his death by transferring his
personal oversight to the Conference of preachers.   The importance of Christian community led to the creation of
"Bands" and the "Classes" as a characteristic form of small
group life in Methodism.   The names were taken over from
the Moravians, but the essence can be claimed as an almost
universal trait and feature of church renewal movements in
those decades.   And for Wesley it meant much that this was
an ecumenical feature and especially that the idea had long
proved effective in the Roman Catholic Church.   We may remember, as Wesley did, the very energetic discipline of the
Societas Jesu (founded 1534) and of the informal societies
called into being by Bérulle and de Renty, of Horneck's religious societies at the Savoy in London, of the ecclesiola in
ecclesia suggested by Spener, the head of Lutheran Pietism,
and used by Count Zinzendorf as legitimation for his organi-
zational forms.   All these analogies have been claimed for
Wesley and the Methodist tradition.   But it does not matter
whether he followed a given model or whether he derived the
pattern directly from early Christianity, from Jesus himself
and his family of disciples.   Wesley himself sometimes ap-

pealed to St. Francis of Assisi and his group as a model of
Christian community. The substantial tradition of Christian
community was in itself meaningful and obliging enough.

How deeply this feeling and longing for Christian community was rooted in Wesley's mind can be seen from various occurrences in his life. He felt happy at Oxford with
the Holy Club. He became nervous when he found himself
isolated in Georgia. Each of his friends was given a different task in the colony--Charles served as Secretary to General Oglethorpe and was located at Frederica; Benjamin Ing-
ham was assigned to the Indian Mission; Charles Delamotte
was partly with him or with Charles. He himself was the
vicar of the parish of Savannah. When Wesley arrived at
Herrnhut in August of 1738, he soon felt very much at home
in the community. However, his encounter with Zinzendorf,
an isolated gentleman of his own type, imposing himself on
his followers, impressed him only for a moment. The reasons for complaint and criticism of the Moravians did not
stem from those weeks spent at Herrnhut itself, but from the
authoritarian position of the Count among his brethren and
from doctrinal points such as Antinomianism, mystical stillness and, as his final conversation with Zinzendorf in September of 1741 reveals, from a different view of perfect or
imperfect Christian holiness and the place of remaining sin
which was related to Antinomianism but not identical with it.
I am also convinced that the unhappy development of Wesley's
marriage had its roots almost exclusively in his close attachment to the life together in his Methodist societies to which
he was committed. No other alliance and loyalty seriously
had a chance. This was more influential than his wrong se-
lection of a wife.

Pastoral care, cura animarum in the sense of Gregory I (ca.540-604), the Roman pontiff and father of the Medieval Papacy, was the basic concern and starting point of Wesley's movement. It seems to me that we cannot easily find another movement in church history which grew by this emphasis into a real church of its own type. We may think of Monasticism, but this movement did not end up in a separate church, not even in medieval Ireland or in ancient Ethiopia--churches where authority was vested in a monastic order. I know, and I even insist on the fact, that Methodism did not originate exclusively on the lines of pastoral care, but it must be stated that this was one of its characteristic features. Wesley stressed pastoral concerns on various occasions, not on principle but in order that fellowship in Christ might become a reality. As he pointed out his followers were often isolated as soon as they had attached themselves to his preaching, and therefore he was committed to take care of them. He stressed pastoral care, not for building up his own Wesleyan Methodist Church, but for helping the people deal with their own real emergency life situations.

Here again we see an important reason why Wesley maintained authority within the movement. By a democratic vote, a clear separation from the Church of England would have been inevitable at a pretty early stage, especially since the Anglican bishops were almost exclusively distant if not hostile. It was Wesley's search for unity and community in the body of Christ which withheld separation from the established church during his lifetime. He agreed in 1784 to unilateral ordinations only because of the emergency situation in North America.

Common life in the body of Christ, for Wesley, finally has an ecumenical dimension. This was undoubtedly a real concern for Wesly from the beginning. The divided state of

Christendom throughout the world moved him from his early
days when he commented briefly on the sad events of Thorn
(Torun) in Poland in 1724. [6] On the other hand, he was free
from prejudice and "catholic" in spirit when, in spite of
clear attachment to the Reformation and even to Luther himself, whom he regarded as the God's champion against Satan
in the eschatological drama, he expressed admiration for Ig-
natius Loyola and the spirit of his society. [7] And in a sense
he was even pleased that he himself was labeled--or libeled
--a Jesuit. [8] His outlook was broad and his horizon wide.
He demonstrated this especially in the field of church history.
In publishing his 50-volume Christian Library (1749-1755) he
created the idea of a library of Christian classics. His library became the direct forerunner of Everyman's Library
in England. From an early age he collected works which he
regarded from a devotional, moral and educational point of
view as essential and offered them as a permanent companion
to the members of the Methodist societies. Thereby he implanted the consciousness of a common Christian heritage
alongside the Bible for Christian nurture. And this came
from the man who pretended and emphasized to be Homo
Unius Libri! [9] He obviously understood Christian literature
as an extension of Holy Scripture. Further he prepared a
new translation and abridgment of the most famous handbook
of Christ's history of his era, Johann Lorenz von Mosheim's
Institutiones Historiae Ecclesiasticae (1726). [10] The number
of tracts which Wesley abridged and published in order to
make them available to his followers in inexpensive editions
is considerably high. And he selected them from every part
of the Christian tradition which he thought valuable, Catholic
and Protestant, Eastern and Western. He translated German
hymns into English and published the first of several ecumen-

ical hymnals as early as his second year in Georgia. [11]   It
was a remarkable fact, perhaps not sufficiently stressed,
that the core of these hymns which he translated early in his
career were not Moravian in origin, but Hallensian.   They
included an important hymn of Paul Gerhardt (ca. 1607-1676),
the orthodox Lutheran poet of the 17th century. [12]

   In his Bible studies Wesley used everything which
seemed helpful for understanding the text.   His "Explanatory
Notes" on the Old Testament (1765) and on the New Testament (1755) are based on former expositors--Hugo Grotius
(1583-1645), the liberal humanist, and especially Johann Al-
brecht Bengel (1687-1752), the conservative pietist.

   As to his relationship and indebtedness to German pietism, it is noteworthy that he did not give himself completely to one of the two main streams.   During his stay as a
missioner in Georgia in 1735-36 he met two different types
of German Pietism.   On the one hand, there were the Moravians represented by Augustus Gottlieb Spangenberg (1704-
1792), David Nitschmann (1696-1772), and Johann Töltschig,
and later by Peter Böhler (1712-1775) and Zinzendorf, not to
mention the important contact with Christian David and Arvid
Gradin at Herrnhut.   On the other hand, Wesley also met in
Georgia Hallensian Pietism represented by Boltzius and Gronau, the young Lutheran ministers of Salzburgers at New
Ebenezer in Georgia.   At that time and later, the antagon-
ism between Halle and Herrnhut was one of the dominant features in pietism in Germany.   Wesley had the unique oppor-
tunity to examine both almost on the same spot, each of
whom under difficult conditions in the wilderness colony had
built up a remarkable Christian community.   This must have
sharpened his eye and helped him to an impartial assessment.   I am inclined to the judgment that in his criticism

of the Moravians, Wesley agreed in major points with the
Hallensians, especially on the complaint about antinomianism.
John Wesley, already in his early days, received a deep and
lasting impression from a testimony of Hallensian piety, i.e.,
Augustus Hermann Francke's tract, "Nicodemus on the Fear
of Man." He read the popular English translation by
Francke's "ambassador" in London, Anton Wilhelm Böhme
(1673-1722), the friend of Isaac Watts and of Henry Newman,
the secretary of the SPCK. Francke's fearless Christian
radicalism, his full obedience to God, his complete honesty
appealed to Wesley and became a formative influence upon
him. Wesley prepared and published an abridged version of
the tract in 1739. [13]

The common life in the body of Christ also demanded
and encouraged social responsibility in a high degree. Social
action proved to become an important characteristic of Methodism. Wesley was concerned about the principal social issues of the day--poverty, education, slavery and the slave
trade, alcoholism, loyalty or independence of the American
colonies, etc. Even where as a conservative he seemed to
be wrong, he took seriously the Christian responsibility to
become involved in public issues. Thus he created--perhaps
indirectly--a socially concerned Christianity in an age of humanitarian endeavor on the lines of the Enlightenment. Subsequently the trade union movement in Britain gained much
from the Methodist lay preachers who for a long period
formed the core of its public speakers.

Now, eighthly, coming to the last, we reach the really
crucial point for determining Wesley's place in church history. He was the first in the whole course of church history
who realized that the task of Christendom in the modern
world is to be defined as mission. Here again Wesley took

his cue from the missionary enterprise to the Gentiles in the
early days of the church.   Wesley went to Georgia expressly
because he wanted to be a missionary to the American Indi-
ans.   He wanted to be in a position to rediscover the original meaning and purpose of the New Testament, which he
clearly recognized as a missionary document.   This insight
is something of highest importance.   I do not know of any
other Christian in the 18th century who had this clear and
distinctive insight.   His conviction that the Word of God, or,
as he often said in accord with the Calvinist tradition, "the
Oracles of God," could reveal its meaning only when it was
actually preached to Gentiles.   This belief in the real presence and power of God's word in the event of preaching
brings Wesley close to Luther.   Church history thus becomes
not merely the record of the church's institutions and leaders,
but the story of the preached word, of its successes and failures through the years in widely different contexts.   Church
history becomes a history of missions not in the sense of
Kenneth Scott Latourette's magnificent series on "the Expansion of Christianity," but in the sense of missionary oppor-
tunities and beginnings, no longer simply by settled pastors
in parishes but also by roving itinerant preachers.

On this point--itinerant preaching--compromise was
not possible.   Anglican bishops and parish clergy claimed
that England was a Christian country and Europe a Christian
continent.   Wesley protested: England, as well as Europe,
was inhabited by hordes of heathens.   Therefore the Church
must start missions by preaching the Gospel at home as well
as at the ends of the earth.   That meant, for Wesley, preaching not only by settled pastors in parishes but, more important, by migrating, itinerant ministers as in the primitive
church.   On this point of evangelistic strategy, Methodism's

conflict with mother church became evident and the rift inevitable.

It was the experience of Georgia, this very short period at the beginning of his ministry, which must not be underestimated in its formative significance on Wesley and the
development of the Methodist evangelistic movement!   Here
Wesley first discovered the missionary nature of the Church,
mission to indifferent Christians who had lost their heritage.
If the church is only a heritage, of mighty deeds in the past
and does not issue in present mission and evangelism, it is
not a true church.   This discovery gave him a unique place
in church history.   He was well prepared for this discovery
by the impact of Bartholomaeus Ziegenbalg's report from
Francke's Danish-Halle mission in southern India, Propagation of the Gospel to the East (1709), on his mother, Susanna.
She had written to her husband, as she told her son later,
that after having read that report she had been able to think
or to speak of little else. [14]   She decided from that very day
(about February 6, 1712) to dedicate for each of her children
an evening of pastoral care by personal conversation about religious subjects.   At that time John had not yet completed his
9th year of age and he was in a stage of great openness to
formative impressions.   Surely this must have been one of his
distinctive experiences.

Summing up, let us state: John Wesley's place in
church history is determined first, by his loyal adherence, if
not unity of theological conviction and religious experience, to
the church in her whole ecumenical tradition as well as to his
native Church of England; secondly, by the coincidence of biography (personal life), personal faith and task, and personal
mission; thirdly, by his insistence on the common life in the
body of Christ which includes ecumenical openness along with

clear theological convictions; fourthly, by his discovery that
the task of Christendom in the modern secular world is to be
understood and practiced as mission, following the example
of the early church's mission to the Gentiles; and fifthly and
lastly, by his ability to undertake this renewal of the church
without becoming a revolutionary or in any way disloyal to his
Anglican tradition, which highly valued the early church and
patristic theology as well as devotional and common life. It
is a combination of all of these factors that qualified him to
leadership of high rank in the history of Christendom.

You will notice that I changed the subject and theme
assigned to me. I have discussed Wesley's place in church
history rather than Wesley's relation to the Christian tradition from a Lutheran perspective. This seems to me to be
meaningful, because John Wesley was able to be loyal to different traditions. He was willing to cross the lines of a divided Christendom. His aim in all of this was to restore
primitive, evangelical, ecumenical Christianity.

NOTES

1. Albert C. Outler, editor, John Wesley (New York: Ox-
    ford University Press, 1964), p. 27.

2. Wesley to Freeborn Garrettson, January 24, 1789 in
    Letters, edited by Telford, VIII, p. 112.

3. "All these days [Wesley wrote in his journal] I scarce
    remember to have opened the Testament, but upon
    some 'great and precious promise.' And I saw more
    than ever that the gospel is in truth but one great
    promise, from the beginning of it to the end. "--June
    4, 1738 in Journal, edited by Curnock, I, p. 482.
    For Wesley's use of the Bible see also his sermon
    "On Corrupting the Word of God" (1727), Works VII,
    468-473; Prefaces to "Explanatory Notes upon the New
    Testament, " (1755) Works XIV, pp. 235-239 and "Ex-

planatory Notes upon the Old Testament," (1765)
Works XIV, pp. 246-253; "A Clear and Concise Dem-
onstration of the Divine Inspiration of the Holy Scripture," Works XI, p. 484; Notes on the New Testament
2 Timothy 3:16.

4. Wesley quotes Gradin's definition of sanctification in his
    "A Plain Account of Christian Perfection," Works XI,
    pp. 369-370; see also Journal II, p. 49.

5. Lionel S. Thornton, The Common Life in the Body of
    Christ (London, Dacre Press, 1942).

6. Wesley to Susannah Wesley, July 29, 1725 in Letters,
    ed. Telford, I, p. 20.

7. Journal, August 16, 1742 in Journal, ed. Curnock, III,
    p. 40.

8. For example see Wesley's second letter to Bishop Lav-
    ington, Works IX, pp. 58-59; see also Journal, Feb-
    ruary 5, 1749 in Journal, edited by Curnock, III, p.
    390.

9. Preface to "Sermons on Several Occasions," 1746 in
    Standard Sermons, edited by Sugden, I, p. 32.

10. A Concise Ecclesiastical History from the Birth of
    Christ to the Beginning of the Present Century (Lon-
    don: John Paramore, 1781), 4 vols. For Wesley's
    comments on Mosheim see Works III, p. 441; p. 303
    and XIV, pp. 297-299.

11. A Collection of Psalms and Hymns (Charlestown, S.C.:
    Lewis Timothy, 1737). See especially "Psalms and
    Hymns for Sunday," numbers XVI, XXVI, and XL and
    "Psalms and Hymns for Wednesday or Friday," num-
    bers XIV and XX.

12. "Ich singe dir mit hertz und mund" ("To Thee I sing
    with heart and mind"). Wesley translated the first
    six of Gerhardt's eighteen verses. For unknown rea-
    sons this translation appears in none of Wesley's
    hymn books. See John L. Nuelsen, John Wesley and
    the German Hymn, translated by Theodore Parry et
    al. (Calverley, England: A. S. Holbrook, 1972), pp.
    52 and 161.

13.   Nicodemus; or, A Treatise on the Fear of Man was
      first published in Bristol in 1739.   Six editions were
      published during Wesley's lifetime.

14.   Journal, August 1, 1742 in Journal, edited by Curnock,
      III, p. 32.

CHAPTER IV

SALVATION TODAY AND WESLEY TODAY

Michael Hurley, S. J.

Somebody once remarked that the three forms in which
thought can be presented are solid, liquid and gas: "the last
for an audience, the second for a book, the first for an Arch-
angel in retreat." It was the Roman Catholic Modernist, ex-
Jesuit and Irishman, George Tyrrell, who made the remark.
It occurs in a letter of his to von Hügel. He is criticizing
the Baron's earlier style as lacking a proper flow of language
and lightness of touch and as being unfit in its Teutonic heav-
iness even for 'the Cherubim and Seraphim.' Tyrrell's particular criticism of von Hügel may indeed be justified but his
general reference to an audience as needing thought presented
to it in the form of gas is hardly complimentary and is certainly less than just. The ideal form of communication,
whatever the medium, would (I suppose) be a combination of
solid, liquid and gas; and this is what I shall try to achieve
--though not without reminding you in advance that the combination may be as intellectually impossible as it is chemi-
cally contradictory.

I have elsewhere described John Wesley as "a man
sent by God at a time when Christianity in these islands
[Britain and Ireland] was for a variety of reasons rather sunk
on its lees and when the frontiers of America, eighty per

cent of which was still uninhabited, were beginning to expand
very rapidly. " His work, I have suggested, was that of pro-
viding "a reforming and missionary agency by means of which
a deep and widespread religious revival took place in Great
Britain and Ireland, and in America such a rapid expansion
of Christianity as 'had not been equalled in Christendom since
the Apostolic Era'. " The question, however, to which I am
here and now invited to address myself assumes Wesley's
significance in the past and inquires about his relevance today, in particular for Roman Catholicism. Fortunately it is
not too difficult to identify the subject which at present con-
stitutes the main focus of interest and concern for the Roman
Catholic Church and indeed for all the Churches. Uppsala
has been followed by Bangkok, Bangkok by Lausanne, Lausanne by the Roman Synod of Bishops, and, more recently,
the fifth Assembly of the World Council of Churches in Nai-
robi. "Salvation Today" has been, is, and will be high on
the agenda of all these meetings. Greatly daring therefore,
I have chosen as the title of this paper: "Salvation Today
and Wesley Today. "

I.   The Vertical and the Horizontal

In this context of "Salvation Today" the first problem
which presents itself concerns the vertical and horizontal dimensions of the Gospel. Is it the Church's missionary task
to save souls, to convert and deepen the faith of individuals?
Or is it also part of the Church's missionary task to save
society: not only to alleviate evil in all its forms but above
all to eradicate evil by pioneering reform of the structures
and systems which are its root cause? Has Wesley any light
to throw on these questions, for Roman Catholics in particular?

What pre-Vatican II Roman Catholics thought about this
problem is well illustrated in the correspondence between
Arnold Lunn and Ronald Knox. "Surely [Lunn wrote], on a
priori grounds it would be reasonable to expect that a Church
which was founded to carry on the work of Christ would have
led this great humanitarian campaign, instead of following re-
luctantly in the rear?" To which Knox's frank reply was:

> I do think it is true, on the whole, that the agita-
> tions which have benefited mankind have been large-
> ly the work of non-Catholics, and indeed non-Chris-
> tians. But then I think the instinct of all Catholic
> saints and philanthropists is to make the best of ex-
> isting conditions, relieving the sufferings of the
> present and leaving the conditions to alter them-
> selves: Providence Row, for example; or all the
> innumerable works of charity set on foot by St. Vin-
> cent de Paul, which did not alter the social institu-
> tions of the French monarchy. I do not boast of
> this, or poke fun (as Dean Inge used to do when we
> were up) at the alliance between Christianity and so-
> cial reform. I only note it as a fact that on the
> whole your non-religious man is a more successful
> reformer, because he can work for the future, with-
> out worrying over the souls of the people who are
> on the streets here and now. [1]

Too many Roman Catholics would still have little difficulty in
seeing themselves in this last revealing sentence of Ronald
Knox. In principle, however, since Vatican II, we would now
agree that Christianity is not a religion of pietism but of
service: that it must also be concerned with the so-called
secular tasks which reform and humanize society. Indeed
there has been such rapid change in both theory and practice
that one of the questions which the Synod of Bishops had on
the agenda for its 1974 meeting reads as follows:

> There are those who describe evangelization as
> though it were something only on the spiritual and
> religious level, meant only to free man from the

bonds of sin. Others however describe Christ as
the new Moses and consider that the Gospel is or-
dered only towards human development, at least at
the present moment of history. One asks whether
one should speak of two finalities (albeit closely
connected ones), or whether both these aspects of
evangelization blend into one. Where should the
emphasis be placed? What is to be said of the
statements: 'The Church promotes the human by
evangelizing' and 'The Church evangelizes by promoting the human'? (Cf. the problems of the theology of politics and of the theology of liberation
and revolution.)

Personally I do not consider that we should allow ourselves to be stampeded either by Germans or by Latin Amer-
icans into thinking that a solution to this theoretical, theological problem is a top priority. Neither would I wish at this
stage to declare with Peter Beyerhaus and "The Frankfurt
Declaration" that social and political involvement is a mere,
if "important accompaniment and authentication of mission."
I do not share the anxieties of those who dwell on the imbal-
ances of Bangkok. I seem to remember that in the early
Church, Council had to succeed Council to correct the doctrinal imbalance of its predecessor. And even if Lausanne
has already followed Bangkok as Chalcedon followed Ephesus,
we do well perhaps to remember that Chalcedon itself was only a stage on the road. In any case our experience to date
seems too little and too short-lived to provide sufficient material for reflection and the consequent elaboration of reliable
theory. It would seem more important at the present junc-
ture that the Church be engaged and be seen to be engaged
both in the work of saving souls and in the work of saving society, rather than that we should know precisely how the two
are connected or whether they are essentially two different
activities at all and not basically one and the same.

This, I suggest, might well be the advice which John
Wesley would give to the Synod of Bishops. It would, I think,
be a typically Wesleyan approach insofar as the emphasis is
put on orthopraxy rather than orthodoxy. Wesley's ideal certainly was "faith which worketh by love" (Gal 5:6) and not
faith which exhausts itself in an "endless jangling about opinions." Our first priority is "to provoke one another to love
and to good works."[2] Orthodoxy must take second place.
"Orthodoxy, or right opinions, is, at best, but a very slender
part of religion, if it can be allowed to be any part of it at
all."[3]

We can hardly imagine John Wesley encouraging our
Synod of Bishops to canonize today's liberation theology. He
would react to much of this in the same way as George Tyrrell (if I may quote him again) reacted to the Liberal Protestantism of his day, "with its bland faith and hope in the present order," its optimism "begotten of faith in this world, not
of faith in the other." He would speak even more disparag-
ingly of certain modern trends than Tyrrell himself did when
he wrote in Christianity at the Crossroads: "The Churches
chatter progress, and the secular and clerical arm are linked
together in the interests of a sanctified worldliness" but in
actual fact the Gospel "stands or falls with faith in another
life, in which the stifled spirit can realize itself in another
order of experience."[4] On the other hand Wesley would be
emphatic in reminding our Bishops that salvation is this-
worldly and not other-worldly. "Salvation," he would insist,
"is not what is frequently understood by that word, the going
to heaven, eternal happiness. It is not the soul's going to
paradise.... It is not a blessing which lies on the other side
of death; or, as we usually speak, in the other world.... It
is not something at a distance: it is a present thing; a bless

ing which, through the free mercy of God, ye are now in possession of. "[5] And Wesley would also take--and make-- the point that Christians must not be so heavenly-minded that they are no earthly good. The Church, he would stress,

> is a body of men compacted together, in order, first, to save each his own soul; then to assist each other in working out their salvation; and, af- terwards, as far as in them lies, to save all men from present and future misery, to overturn the kingdom of Satan, and set up the kingdom of Christ .... And this ought to be the continued care and endeavour of every member of His Church. [6]

> [Love of neighbour, Wesley would also stress] con- tinually incites us to do good as we have time and opportunity; to do good, in every possible kind and in every possible degree, to all men. [7]

> The same love is productive of all right actions. It leads him [the Christian] into an earnest and steady discharge of all social offices, of whatever is due to relations of every kind: to his friends, to his country and to any particular community whereof he is a member. It prevents his willingly hurting or grieving any man. It guides him into an uniform practice of justice and mercy, equally extensive with the principle whence it flows. It constrains him to do all possible good, of every possible kind, to all men; and makes him invariably resolved in every circumstance of life to do that, and that only, to others, which supposing he were himself in the same situation, he would desire they should do to him. [8]

We know how Wesley himself practiced what he preached; and it would impress and influence the Synod of Bishops. True to his convictions, he went around doing good, "healing all that were oppressed by the devil. " The man whose overriding concern was "to reform the nation by spread- ing Scriptural holiness over the Land" was in fact concerned not only with people's spiritual welfare but also with their physical, mental and economic welfare. He distributed pills

and tracts.   He established clinics and schools and facilities
for interest-free loans.   He joined in condemning slavery as
well as smuggling, bribery and corruption.   He could pen and
publish "Thoughts on the Present Scarcity of Provisions" and
even seem to suggest that only government control over some
aspects of the economy could remedy poverty.   He did of
course forbid "meddling in politics" but his followers had
been taken as "Papists in disguise in the pay of the Pretend-
er."   Clearly he was no radical.   His outlook was to a large
extent time-conditioned, with the result that though he protested, for instance, against prison conditions, he issued no
"Thoughts on Prison Reform."   It may be true that his most
enlightened social attitudes owed much to Moravian and Quaker
influence; that his "Thoughts on Slavery" was a pirated
abridgment of a Quaker work.   What matters most is that the
man who told his Helpers they had "nothing to do but to save
souls" was also intent on saving society, and that he saw, in
some instances at least, that the way to do so was to change
structures.   Later Methodism may (in the words of The History of American Methodism) have "swallowed uncritically the
moldy fallacy that if we develop Christian individuals society
will thereby become Christian."   Wesley himself was on the
whole more discerning than that.   He would have considered
the spiritual and social forms of Methodism to be "comple-
mentary and mutually necessary," as George Tyrrell thought
the "mystical and social forms of Modernism" were.   He
would have agreed with Tyrrell that "the Christian faith ...
balances an absolute detachment from the interests of the
world" by a "provisional attachment to them" and that, "far,
then, from relaxing moral effort for the alleviation of earth's
misery, the Christian faith, rightly apprehended, intensifies
and purifies," though without making "earth our heaven, and
humanity our God."[9]

There is enough in John Wesley, in his blind spots
and in his insights, to warn the Roman Synod of Bishops
against either of the extremes in their approach to "Salvation
Today." More importantly, there is much in him to encour-
age our Bishops to take in general a both/and rather than an
either/or attitude. The relationship between the vertical and
horizontal dimensions of the Gospel would seem to be another
example of the fact that Christianity is an unseen harmony of
seeming opposites. With Visser 't Hooft, speaking at Uppsala, we must continue to maintain that:

> A Christianity which has lost its vertical dimension
> has lost its salt and is not only insipid in itself,
> but useless for the world. But a Christianity which
> would use the vertical preoccupation as a means to
> escape from its responsibility for and in the com-
> mon life of man is a denial of the incarnation, of
> God's love for the world manifested in Christ. [10]

II.   The Salvific Role of Other Religions

We turn now to the most difficult of all the problems
raised by the Salvation Today debate: what should the attitude of Christians be to men of other faiths and to their religions? The stance in this matter of Peter Beyerhaus and
"The Frankfurt Declaration" (1971) is clearly negative:

> We therefore oppose the false teaching (which is
> spreading in the ecumenical movement since the
> Third General Assembly of the World Council of
> Churches in New Delhi) that Christ himself is
> anonymously so evident in world religions, histori-
> cal changes, and revolutions that man can encounter
> him and find salvation in him without the direct
> news of the Gospel....

> We therefore oppose the universalistic idea that in
> the crucifixion and resurrection of Jesus Christ all
> men of all times are already born again and al-
> ready have peace with him, irrespective of their

> knowledge of the historical saving activity of God
> or belief in it....
>
> We therefore reject the false teaching that the non-
> christian religions and world views are also ways
> of salvation similar to belief in Christ.
>
> We refute the idea that 'Christian presence' among
> the adherents to the world religions and a give-
> and-take dialogue with them are substitutes for a
> proclamation of the Gospel which aims at conver-
> sion.   Such dialogues simply establish good points
> of contact for missionary communication. [11]

Some writers speak of a "contrast between Roman
Catholic and Protestant positions" with regard to the salvific
role of other religions.   According to one (John B. Carman):

> Ecumenical discussion in Western Europe between
> Roman Catholics and Protestants is now widespread.
> It is therefore all the more striking that recent
> thinking about 'religion and the religions' among
> Catholic and Protestant theologians should veer off
> so sharply in opposite directions, Roman Catholics
> affirming the value of human religion in general
> and other religions in particular in the divine econ-
> omy of salvation, while many neo-Reformation theo-
> logians and those influenced by them have regarded
> 'religion' as largely or even wholly opposed to
> Christian faith. [12]

It is as a result of this trend that the Synod of Bishops in
Rome asked itself: "What should one think of the theories of
'anonymous Christians,' of 'implicit faith sufficient for salvation,' of 'salvation without the Gospel', etc.?   May it be said
that non-Christian religions have a salvific value in themselves (not only as forms of preparation for the Gospel) and
that the Gospel is only one way of salvation, though a privi-
leged one?   Do you think that this interpretation [of Vatican
II] can be reconciled with the absolute and unique newness of
the Gospel?" In the context of this paper the question to
which we must now address ourselves is: What help can

John Wesley give us as we struggle with this aspect of the "Salvation Today" problem.   In what follows I wish to suggest that he can help us with his theology of prevenient grace.

I begin with a quotation from a letter of John Wesley. The words are actually the words of a Quaker but they are followed immediately by the statement: "in these points there is no difference between Quakerism and Christianity."

> All mankind is fallen and dead, deprived of the sensation of this inward testimony of God, and subject to the power and nature of the devil, while they abide in their natural state.   And hence not only their words and deeds, but all their imaginations, are evil perpetually in the sight of God.
>
> God out of His infinite love hath so loved the world that He gave His only Son, to the end that whosoever believeth on Him might have everlasting life.   And He enlighteneth every man that cometh into the world, as He tasted death for every man.
>
> The benefit of the death of Christ is not only extended to such as have the distinct knowledge of His death and sufferings, but even unto those who are inevitably excluded from this knowledge.   Even these may be partakers of the benefit of His death, though ignorant of the history, if they suffer His grace to take place in their hearts, so as of wicked men to become holy. [13]

This passage does not contain the term prevenient grace, nor what I take to be its equivalent, "preventing grace."   Neither does it indicate what the reality of prevenient or preventing grace might be.   It does, however, point to the context, the basis and the missionary implications of this Wesleyan notion.

The context--partly at least--is the doctrine of original sin.   John Wesley yields to no man in his acceptance of the total depravity of fallen human nature.   The first paragraph of the passage just quoted is a relatively mild description.   Fallen man is "indeed all sin, a mere lump of ungodli-

ness,"[14] "altogether corrupt and abominable, more than it is
possible for tongue to express."[15] But the worst that can
be said of fallen human nature is, for Wesley, only half the
truth. Besides the Fall there is the fact of the Atonement:
there is Christ, "the true light that enlightens every man."

   According to Wesley the Atonement of Christ means
that there is--and since the fall of Adam always has been--
grace for all and in all "to balance the corruption of nature."[16] In his sermon "On Working Out Our Own Salvation"
he writes:

> For allowing that all the souls of men are dead in
> sin by nature, this excuses none, seeing there is
> no man that is in a state of mere nature; there is
> no man, unless he has quenched the Spirit, that is
> wholly void of the grace of God. No man living is
> entirely destitute of what is vulgarly called natural
> conscience. But this is not natural: It is more
> properly termed, preventing grace. Every man has
> a greater or less measure of this, which waiteth
> not for the call of man. Every one has, sooner or
> later, good desires; although the generality of men
> stifle them before they can strike deep root, or pro-
> duce any considerable fruit. Every one has some
> measure of that light, some faint glimmering ray,
> which, sooner or later, more or less, enlightens
> every man that cometh into the world. And every
> one, unless he be one of the small number whose
> conscience is seared as with a hot iron, feels more
> or less uneasy when he acts contrary to the light
> of his own conscience. So that no man sins because
> he has not grace, but because he does not use the
> grace which he hath.[17]

Here again, as so often, we hear an echo of the Prologue of
St. John's Gospel. Here too we find that the reality corresponding to Wesley's prevenient grace is closely associated
with conscience. The frequent allusions to the ninth verse of
St. John's Prologue can leave us in no doubt that this verse
provides John Wesley with the immediate basis for his theol-

ogy of prevenient grace. We may also remember that this
verse influenced Vatican II's "Declaration on the Relationship of the Church to Non-Christian Religions," where it
is stated that these religions "often reflect a ray of that
Truth which enlightens all men."[18] It is not yet clear, however, what the connection is for Wesley between prevenient
grace and conscience, or, more importantly, what the connection is for him between prevenient grace and salvation.

This latter connection becomes clearer if we turn
again to his sermon "On Working Out Our Own Salvation" and
read the following passage on the stages of salvation:

> Salvation begins with what is usually termed (and
> very properly) preventing grace; including the first
> wish to please God, the first dawn of light concern-
> ing his will, and the first slight transient convic-
> tion of having sinned against him. All these imply
> some tendency towards life; some degree of salva-
> tion; the beginning of a deliverance from a blind,
> unfeeling heart, quite insensible of God and the
> things of God. Salvation is carried on by convinc-
> ing grace, usually in Scripture termed repentance;
> which brings a larger measure of self-knowledge,
> and a farther deliverance from the heart of stone.
> Afterwards we experience the proper Christian sal-
> vation; whereby, 'through grace,' we are 'saved by
> faith'; consisting of those two grand branches, justi-
> fication and sanctification.[19]

Here we find no mention of conscience, but another sermon
on "The Scripture Way of Salvation" does link the three (salvation, prevenient grace and conscience) as follows:

> The salvation which is here spoken of [Eph. 2:8--
> 'Ye are saved through faith'] might be extended to
> the entire work of God, from the first dawning of
> grace in the soul, till it is consummated in glory.
> If we take this in its utmost extent, it will include
> all that is wrought in the soul by what is frequently
> termed 'natural conscience,' but more properly,
> 'preventing grace'; all the drawings of the Father--

> the desires after God, which, if we yield to them,
> increase more and more; all that light wherewith
> the Son of God 'enlighteneth every one that cometh
> into the world'--showing every man 'to do justly,
> to love mercy, and to walk humbly with his God';
> all the convictions which His Spirit, from time to
> time, works in every child of man--although it is
> true, the generality of men stifle them as soon as
> possible, and after a while forget, or at least deny,
> that they ever had them at all. [20]

It would seem to follow from these passages that the reality
corresponding to prevenient grace is not so much conscience
simpliciter but conscience insofar as it is drawn by the Father of our Lord Jesus Christ, illuminated by the Word Incar-
nate, stirred by the Spirit of Jesus and thus enabled, in the
same Spirit, to "react" in repentance and faith leading to
justification and sanctification.   Prevenient grace, so interpreted, has much more in common with the fifth and sixth
chapters of the Tridentine Decree on Justification than it has
with Karl Rahner's "supernatural existentiale. "[21]

Between the various stages of salvation sketched in
outline above there is a certain continuity and, for Wesley,
man's "reaction" is vital.   Today we should say "response"
but the term "reaction" is typically Wesleyan.   (The editor
of the Standard Sermons [I, p. 304, note 1] tells us that the
Oxford English Dictionary quotes Wesley as the earliest example of the use of "reaction" in the sense of "the influence
which a thing, acted upon by another, exercises in return upon the agent," as distinct from the older meaning: "repul-
sion exerted in opposition to impact of pressure. "[22]   What
Wesley says of the believer we may, I suggest, apply to the
sinner cooperating in the process of his salvation:

> [He] continually receives into his soul the breath of
> life from God, the gracious influence of His Spirit,
> and continually renders it back.... by faith [he]

> perceives the continual actings of God upon his
> spirit, and, by a kind of spiritual reaction returns
> the grace he receives.... For it plainly appears,
> God does not continue to act upon the soul, unless
> the soul reacts upon God. He prevents us indeed
> with the blessings of His goodness.... [But] He
> will not continue to breathe into our soul, unless
> our soul breathes toward Him again. [23]

But in what sense, if any, may we say of the repenting sinner as of the believing Christian that it is by faith that he
"reacts" to God's grace? Wesley, himself, states that faith
is already operative in the early stages of the sinner's salvation, but it is, in his own words, "a low species of faith,
i.e., a supernatural sense of an offended God."[24] It is not
yet faith in Christ and in the Gospel. It is not yet the saving
fiducial faith which must be preceded by repentance. This
saving faith, he tells us, is:

> A sure trust in the mercy of God, through Christ
> Jesus. It is a confidence in a pardoning God. It
> is a divine evidence or conviction that 'God was in
> Christ, reconciling the world to Himself, not imput-
> ing to them their former 'trespasses'; and, in par-
> ticular, that the Son of God hath loved me and given
> Himself for me; and that I, even I, am now recon-
> ciled to God by the Blood of the cross. [25]

The initial faith of repentance in reaction to prevenient and
convincing grace is not however such a "low species" of faith
that it cannot provide what Wesley calls "foretastes of joy,
of peace, of love and those not delusive, but really from God
... [and] may be a [degree] of long-suffering, of gentleness,
of fidelity, meekness, temperance (not a shadow thereof, but
a real degree, by the preventing grace of God)."[26] It would
seem that Wesley does not wish us to distinguish too sharply
his various stages of salvation, nor, indeed, to exclude fiducial faith entirely even from repentance.

Whether or not this interpretation be valid, however,

Wesley holds (as we saw in the passage quoted earlier) that:

> the benefit of the death of Christ [everlasting life]
> is not only extended to such as have the distinct
> knowledge of His death and sufferings, but even un-
> to those who are inevitably excluded from this
> knowledge. Even these may be partakers of the
> benefit of His death, though ignorant of the history,
> if they suffer His grace to take place in their
> hearts, so as of wicked men to become holy. [27]

Wesley is quite definite in stating (what the fifth and sixth
chapters of the Tridentine Decree on Justification do not
state) that "no man living is without some preventing grace,
and every degree of grace is a degree of life."[28] But prevenient grace alone hardly provides us with an adequate ex-
planation of his conviction about the possibility of salvation
for those who do not know Christ. The Conference of 1746
considered the problem. It stressed the concept of "sincerity" which was defined as "willingness to know and do the
will of God." And to the question, "But can it be received
that God has any regard to the sincerity of an unbeliever?"
it answered: "Yes, so much that if he persevere therein,
God will infallibly give him faith."[29] The following year the
Conference also wrestled with the problem:

> Men may have many good tempers and a blameless
> life (speaking in a loose sense) by nature and hab-
> it, with preventing grace, and yet be utterly void
> of faith and the love of God. 'Tis scarce possible
> for us to know all the circumstances relating to
> such persons, so as to judge certainly concerning
> them.
>
> But this we know, that [if] Christ is not revealed
> in them, they are not yet Christian believers.
>
> But what becomes of them then, suppose they die
> in this state? That is a supposition not to be
> made. They cannot die in this state. They must
> go backward or foward. If they continue to seek,

> they will surely find righteousness, peace and joy
> in the Holy Ghost. [30]

These answers surely imply that prevenient grace can flow
into saving grace.   Indeed, only insofar as it can do so,
does it seem possible to envisage with John Wesley the salvation of those who do not hear of Christ.   But does this
possibility not also suppose (what Wesley accepts) that God
was revealed to be, but did not become, our Saviour in the
life, death and glorification of Jesus?   Is this supposition not
required in order to be able to consider that those without
knowledge of Christ can have that "confidence in a pardoning
God" which is of the essence of saving faith?

It seems to follow that Wesley's theology of prevenient grace does imply the possibility of salvation for non-
Christian individuals.   Before passing on, however, we must
ask: did Wesley's "optimism of grace" allow him in fact to
envisage the universality or majority of mankind as saved?
The answer here must be negative.   "Every one," we have
already found him stating, "has, sooner or later, good de-
sires; although the generality of men stifle them before they
can strike deep root, or produce any considerable fruit."[31]
This same pessimistic view finds frequent expression, notably perhaps in his sermons "Upon Our Lord's Sermon on the
Mount" and, very strikingly, in his "short, plain, infallible
rule" for Methodists: "be singular, or be damned."[32]   Before going to Georgia he entertained high hopes of "the heathen" as "fit to receive the gospel in its simplicity ... as
humble, willing to learn, and eager to do the will of God."[33]
In the event, however, he was disillusioned and wrote in his
Journal that "they show no inclination to learn anything, but
least of all Christianity; being full as opinionated of their own
parts and wisdom, as either modern Chinese, or ancient

Romans. "[34]   Wesley's standards of holiness were, of course,
high and he is aware that "the more we grow in grace, the
more do we see of the desperate wickedness of our heart, "[35]
that, indeed, "all that are convinced of sin undervalue themselves in every respect. "[36]   But does the saint's undervaluing of himself involve an undervaluing of others also?   Even
allowing for the evangelist's need to exaggerate, Wesley's
firm views on the general corruption of mankind seem at
odds with his "optimism of grace. "

With regard to the salvific role of other religions, we
do have a letter of Wesley, written before he left for Georgia in 1735, which shows him hoping "to learn the true sense
of the gospel of Christ by preaching it to the heathen. "[37]
But no one who knows his Wesley will expect what follows to
anticipate in any way the views of a Rahner or a Panikkar.
There are, however, aspects of his theology which would
seem to make possible a positive approach to non-Christian
communities as well as to non-Christian individuals.   Wesley recognizes many means of grace and it should be mentioned here en passant that he considers the eucharist as a
"converting ordinance" as "ordained by God to be a means
of conveying to men either preventing, or justifying, or
sanctifying grace, according to their several necessities. "[38]
For Wesley, however, the law--the moral law--is a means
of fundamental importance.   Without the law there is "no
proper means, either of bringing us to faith, or of stirring
up that gift of God in our soul. "[39]   He has to emphasize
that the law is not abolished for the believer, that it is "the
grand means whereby the blessed Spirit prepares the believer
for larger communications of the life of God. "[40]   But the
first use of the law is to bring sinners to repentance: "It
is the ordinary method of the Spirit of God to convict sinners

by the law. It is this which, being set home on the conscience, generally breaketh the rocks in pieces."[41] The per-
tinent question, therefore, for our present purpose is: what,
if anything, may be found in John Wesley's theology which
would enable us to consider non-Christian religions as, to
some extent, embodiments of the law?

Here the fact that Wesley holds the universality of
prevenient grace is relevant and also the related fact that he
considers all men since the Fall to be under the covenant of
grace established by God in Christ. More immediately relevant, perhaps, is Wesley's emphasis on religion as social
and not solitary. This is a point he makes about Christianity in particular. The social character of Christianity is not,
however, for Wesley one of its distinctive features.

> Men [he writes] who did fear God, and desire the
> happiness of their fellow creatures, have, in every
> age, found it needful to join together, in order to
> oppose the works of darkness, to spread the knowl-
> edge of God their Saviour, and to promote His king-
> dom upon earth. Indeed He Himself has instructed
> them so to do. From the time that men were upon
> the earth, He hath taught them to join together in
> His service, and has united them in one body by
> one Spirit.[42]

Wesley's attitude to the observances and structures of non-
Christian religions, of course, will be similar to his attitude to those of the Christian religion: "They are good in
their place; just so far as they are, in fact, subservient to
true religion."[43] On his own principles we today can see
much in non-Christian religions which is in fact "subservient
to true religion." We can, with Vatican II, see them as often reflecting "a ray of that Truth which enlightens all
men."[44] In any case we must apply not only to individuals
but also to communities, and not only to Christian but also

to non-Christian communities, the spirit at least of Wesley's
sermons entitled "A Caution against Bigotry" and "Catholic
Spirit." Here Wesley states:

> Every one is either on God's side, or on Satan's.
> Are you on God's side? Then you will not only not
> forbid any man that casts out devils, but you will
> labour, to the uttermost of your power, to forward
> him in the work. ... What if I were to see a Pap-
> ist, an Arian, a Socinian, casting out devils? If
> I did, I could not forbid even him, without convict-
> ing myself of bigotry. Yea, if it could be supposed
> that I should see a Jew, a Deist, or a Turk, doing
> the same, were I to forbid him either directly or
> indirectly, I should be no better than a bigot still
> .... Encourage whomsoever God is pleased to em-
> ploy, to give himself wholly up thereto [and say to
> him], so far as in conscience thou canst (retaining
> still thy own opinions, and thy own manner of wor-
> shipping God), join with me in the work of God;
> and let us go on hand in hand. [45]

Surely it is only insofar as we do in fact cooperate in
this spirit with other religions that we can be in a position
to discern how much God is using them for his saving purpose and in what ways and to what extent we can grow up together with them "into him who is the head, into Christ."

NOTES

1. Ronald Knox, Difficulties, Being a Correspondence about
   the Catholic Religion between Ronald Knox and Arnold
   Lunn, new ed. (London: Eyre & Spottiswoode, 1952),
   p. 27.

2. John Wesley's Letter to a Roman Catholic, edited by
   Michael Hurley (Dublin: Geoffrey Chapman and Epworth House, 1968), p. 55.

3. "A Plain Account of the People Called Methodists,"
   1748, Works, VIII, p. 249.

4. George Tyrrell, Christianity at the Cross-Roads (London: Longmans, Green & Co., 1910).

5. "The Scripture Way of Salvation," 1765, Standard Sermons, II, pp. 444-445.

6. "The Reformation of Manners," 1763, Standard Sermons, II, pp. 482-483.

7. "The Law Established Through Faith; Discourse II," 1750, Standard Sermons, II, p. 81.

8. "A Plain Account of Genuine Christianity," 1753 in John Wesley, edited by Albert Outler, p. 185.

9. George Tyrrell, op. cit.

10. W. A. Visser 't Hooft, "The Mandate of the Ecumenical Movement," in The Uppsala Report 1968, Official Report of the 4th Assembly of the World Council of Churches, Uppsala, July 4-20, 1968, edited by Norman Goodall (Geneva: World Council of Churches, 1968), p. 318.

11. "The Frankfurt Declaration," in Won Yong Ji, "Evangelization and Humanization," Concordia Theological Monthly, vol. XLII, no. 3 (March, 1971), 165-166. On the views of Peter Beyerhaus, see for example, his Bangkok '73: The Beginning or the End of World Mission? (Grand Rapids, Mich.: Zondervan Publishing House, 1974).

12. John B. Carman, "Continuing Tasks in inter-Religious Dialogue," Ecumenical Review, XXII, No. 3 (July, 1970), p. 200.

13. John Wesley to Thomas Whitehead?, February 10, 1748, Letters, edited by Telford, II, pp. 117-118.

14. "The Righteousness of Faith," 1742, Standard Sermons, I, p. 141.

15. "The Spirit of Bondage and Adoption," 1743, Standard Sermons, I, p. 187.

16. "The Doctrine of Original Sin," 1756, Works, IX, p. 268.

17.   "On Working Out Our Own Salvation," Works, VI, p.
      512.

18.   "Declaration on the Relationship of the Church to Non-
      Christian Religions," in The Documents of Vatican II,
      edited by Walter M. Abbot (New York: Guild Press,
      1966), p. 662.

19.   "On Working Out Our Own Salvation," Works, VI, p.
      509.

20.   "The Scripture Way of Salvation," 1765, Standard Ser-
      mons, II, p. 445.

21.   Karl Rahner, Theological Investigations (London: Dar-
      ton, Longman, & Todd, 1969), VI, pp. 390-398.

22.   Edward H. Sugden, ed., Standard Sermons, I, p. 304,
      note 1.

23.   "The Great Privilege of Those That Are Born of God,"
      Standard Sermons, I, pp. 304, 312.

24.   "Minutes of the Conference," June 25, 1744, Publica-
      tions of the Wesley Historical Society, No. 1, London,
      The Society, 1896, p. 8; also in John Wesley, edited
      by Albert Outler, p. 137.

25.   "The Way to the Kingdom," Standard Sermons, I, p.
      160.

26.   "The Witness of the Spirit," Standard Sermons, II, pp.
      358-359.

27.   John Wesley to Thomas Whitehead?, February 10, 1748,
      Letters, edited by Telford, II, 118.

28.   John Wesley to John Mason, November 21, 1776,
      Letters, edited by Telford, VI, p. 239.

29.   "Minutes of the Conference," May 13, 1746, Publica-
      tions of the Wesley Historical Society, No. 1, Lon-
      don, The Society, 1896, p. 31; also in John Wesley,
      edited by Albert Outler, p. 157.

30.   "Minutes of the Conference," June 16, 1747, Publica-
      tions of the Wesley Historical Society, No. 1, Lon-

don, The Society, 1896, p. 42; also in John Wesley, edited by Albert Outler, p. 167.

31. "On Working Out Our Own Salvation," Works, VI, 512, also 509.

32. "Upon Our Lord's Sermon on the Mount, Discourse XI," Standard Sermons, I, p. 541.

33. John Wesley to Dr. Burton, October 10, 1735, Letters, edited by Telford, I, p. 188.

34. Journal, December 2, 1737, edited by Curnock, I, p. 409.

35. "Upon Our Lord's Sermon on the Mount, Discourse I," Standard Sermons, I, p. 329.

36. "Minutes of Several Conversations between the Rev. Mr. Wesley and Others, 1744-1789," (The Large Minutes) Works, VIII, p. 388.

37. John Wesley to Dr. Burton, October 10, 1735, Letters, edited by Telford, I, p. 188.

38. Journal, June 28, 1740, edited by Telford, II, p. 361; "The Means of Grace," Standard Sermons, I, p. 251.

39. "The Law Established Through Faith, Discourse I," Standard Sermons, II, p. 60.

40. "The Original, Nature, Property, and Use of the Law," Standard Sermons, II, p. 53.

41. Ibid., p. 52.

42. "Sermon Preached Before the Society for the Reformation of Manners," 1763, Standard Sermons, II, p. 482.

43. "The Way to the Kingdom," Standard Sermons, I, p. 149.

44. "Declaration on the Relationship of the Church to Non-Christian Religions," in Documents of Vatican II, edited by Walter M. Abbott (New York: Guild Press, 1966), p. 662.

45. "A Caution Against Bigotry," Standard Sermons, II, pp.
    122, 124; "Catholic Spirit," Standard Sermons, II, p.
    141.

CHAPTER V

THE OXFORD EDITION OF WESLEY'S WORKS
AND ITS TEXT

Frank Baker

As some of you know from experience, and as others may reasonably surmise, I have written on Wesley's Works before. Three times, in 1970, 1971, and 1972, I fulfilled requests for articles surveying the project.[1] Each of these was written from a slightly different angle, but covered the same basic material. And here we are again, in 1974, on the eve of the publication of our first volume. On this occasion I propose to divide what I have to say into two parts: first (for those who have miraculously escaped reading about the project earlier), a compressed summary of the Oxford Edition as a whole; and secondly, something quite new, a somewhat more detailed study of one of its more important features, the recovery of a scholarly text, and what this has to tell us about Wesley.

Perhaps I can best begin by quoting from the preamble to each unit, prepared by the Board of Directors:

> This edition of the works of John Wesley reflects the quickened interest in the heritage of Christian thought that has characterized both ecumenical churchmanship and dominant theological perspectives during the last half-century. A fully critical presentation of his writings has long been

117

a desideratum in order to furnish documentary
sources illustrating his contributions to both catholic and evangelical Christianity.

Several scholars, notably Professor Albert C.
Outler, Professor Franz Hildebrandt, Dean Merri-
mon Cuninggim, and Dean Robert E. Cushman, discussed the possibility of such an edition.   Under
the leadership of Dean Cushman, a Board of Directors was formed in 1960, composed of the deans of
four sponsoring theological schools of Methodist-re-
lated universities in the United States (Drew, Duke,
Emory, and Southern Methodist).   They appointed
an Editorial Committee to formulate plans, and enlisted an international and interdenominational team
of scholars for the 'Wesley's Works Editorial Project.'   The Delegates of the Oxford University
Press agreed to undertake publication.

The works were divided into units of cognate material, with a separate editor (or joint editors) responsible for each unit.   Dr. Frank Baker was appointed textual editor for the whole project, with
responsibility for supplying each unit editor with a
collated critical text for his consideration and use.
The text seeks to represent Wesley's thought in its
fullest and most deliberate expression, in so far as
this can be determined from the available evidence.
Substantive variant readings in any British edition
published during Wesley's lifetime are shown in the
appendixes of the units, preceded by a summary of
the problem faced and the solutions reached in the
complex task of securing and presenting Wesley's
text.   The aim throughout is to enable Wesley to be
read with maximum ease and understanding, and
with minimal intrusion by the editor.

It was decided that the edition should include all
Wesley's original or mainly original prose works,
together with one volume devoted to his Collection
of Hymns for the Use of the People Called Methodists, and another to his extensive work as editor
and publisher of extracts from the writings of others.   An essential feature of the project is a bibliography outlining the historical settings of over 450
items published by Wesley and his brother Charles,
sometimes jointly, sometimes separately.   The bib-

liography also offers full analytical data for identifying each of the 2,000 editions published during
the lifetime of John Wesley, and notes the location
of copies. An index is supplied for each unit, and
a general index for the whole edition.

During the decade 1961-1970, planning was carried forward by the editorial Committee under the
chairmanship of Dean Joseph D. Quillian, Jr. International conferences were convened in 1966 and
1970, bringing together all available unit editors
with the committee, who thus completed their task
of achieving a common mind upon editorial principles and procedures.... Other sponsoring bodies
were successively added to the original four: The
Board of Higher Education and Ministry and The
Commission on Archives and History of the United
Methodist Church, and Boston University School of
Theology.

Financial support has also been given by and will still be
needed from many private individuals and foundations to meet
the cost of the editorial processes, estimated at about
$250,000.

Both in range and size the new edition will be far
larger than the 14 volumes prepared by Thomas Jackson,
1829-31, which remains the best available edition. The units,
volume numbers, and editors, are as follows:

I.   Sermons on Several Occasions, Vols. 1-4, Prof. Albert
      C. Outler, Southern Methodist University, Dallas.
      (This includes new sermons from manuscript sources.)

II.   Explanatory Notes upon the New Testament, Vols. 5-6,
      Prof. John Lawson, Emory University, Atlanta.

III. The Hymnbook, Vol. 7, Dr. Franz Hildebrandt, of Ed-
      inburgh, formerly of Drew, with Dr. Oliver A. Beck-
      erlegge of Cheshunt, England, and Prof. James O.
      Dale, of McMaster University, Hamilton, Ontario.

IV.   Prayers Private and Public, Vol. 8, Rev. A. Raymond
      George of Wesley College, Bristol, England (who will

edit Wesley's Sunday Service of the Methodists), and
Rev. Gordon S. Wakefield, of Manchester, England.

V.   The Methodist Societies: History, Nature and Design,
Vol. 9, Prof. J. Hamby Barton, of Southwestern Col-
lege Winfield, Kansas, and Rev. Rupert E. Davies, of
Bristol, England.

The Methodist Societies: The Conference, Vol. 10 (including all the annual Minutes and the Large Minutes),
Dr. John C. Bowmer and Rev. Norman P. Goldhawk,
both of London, England.

VI.   Doctrinal Writings: The Appeals to Men of Reason and
Religion, Vol. 11, Prof. Gerald R. Cragg, of Andover
Newton Theological School, Newton Center, Mass.
(Published February 1976.)

Doctrinal Writings: Theological Treatises, Vol. 12,
Prof. John Deschner, of Southern Methodist University, Dallas.

Doctrinal Writings: The Defence of Christianity, Vol.
13, Bishop William R. Cannon, of Atlanta.

VII.   Pastoral, Ethical, and Instructional Writings, Vols. 14-
15, Prof. A. Lamar Cooper, of Southern Methodist
University, Dallas.

VIII.   Natural Philosophy and Medicine, Vol. 16, editor not
yet appointed.

IX.   Editorial Works, Vol. 17, Prof. T. Walter Herbert, of
the University of Florida, Gainesville.

X.   Journal and Diaries, Vols. 18-24, Prof. W. Reginald
Ward, of Durham University, England, and Prof. Rich-
ard P. Heitzenrater, of Centre College of Kentucky,
Danville, Kentucky.

XI.   Letters, Vols. 25-31, Prof. Frank Baker, of Duke University, Durham, N.C.

XII.   Bibliography, Vols. 32-3, Prof. Baker.

XIII.   General Index and Miscellanea, Vol. 34, Mr. John
Vickers, of Bognor Regis, England.

The unit editors are charged with the task of helping the reader to understand and appreciate Wesley's text. Each unit will contain a scholarly introduction placing the works in that unit in their historical setting, and showing their significance in Christian life and thought. There will also be a brief introduction to the major individual items in each unit. Supporting these introductions will be footnotes identifying quotations, persons, events, literary usages, and the like. There may also be appendixes of relevant material in addition to the one depicting the textual history and listing the variant readings in each work.

Although this may not seem important to the general reader, in comparison with the general editorial assistance offered, a major contribution of the new edition is the securing of an accurate text. The general reader may also be pardoned for not regarding analytical bibliography and textual criticism as exhilarating pursuits--or even pursuits that are readily comprehensible. The concentrated and prolonged study of minutiae offers many a dull moment. Compared to that of the bibliographer or textual editor, the task of historian or theologian is a joy-ride. I should really say bibliographer and textual editor, for the one must know the problems and needs and tools and purposes of the other, if the end product, the text itself, is to be satisfactory. And yet, they are essential, or a joint bibliographer/textual editor is essential, to any major venture in publishing the works of any historical figure. Every scholarly household should maintain at least one. For he--and here I am trying to straddle the sexist fence--he is the handmaid of higher learning.

Thomas Jackson's edition, which has been reprinted thirty or forty times, was based largely on Wesley's later editions, especially those which bore his manuscript correc-

tions. Nehemiah Curnock's valuable edition of the Journal
also used later editions, conflating their text with the manuscript accounts which survive for some of the earlier passages. Curnock heeded the advice of Richard Green, that
because of its inaccuracies the first edition should be "prac-
tically discarded."

In preparing this new edition, however, the Editorial
Board believed that it was essential to explore the facts more
fully than had ever been done before. First we tried to se-
cure every work prepared by Wesley in every edition published during his lifetime, with the special intention of dis-
covering any alterations for which he might have been responsible. (The original manuscripts of his works seem to
have been destroyed upon publication, and only two sets of
proof sheets have survived.)[2] One edition of each work (usually the first), was typed out, and all the other editions, together with any printed errata or manuscript revisions, were
then collated with it, and the variant readings entered up,
using letter symbols to indicate the editions in which each
variant occurred. A careful study of the patterns of occurrence of these readings, more especially of obvious errors,
enabled us to determine the relationships between the different editions, and to produce for each publication a stemma
depicting the genealogical descent of its text. This same
process also indicated clearly which editions underwent major
revisions of such a character that they must surely have been
carried out by Wesley himself. It also became clear that
many variants were introduced by the fallibility of printers,
and by the idiosyncrasies of the sub-editors or proofreaders
to whom Wesley regularly entrusted the care of his literary
productions, especially in their later editions. For many
careless, infelicitous, or unnecessary alterations, however,

Wesley himself was responsible.

The result of this lengthy and arduous research was to throw us back for the most reliable text away from Wesley's latest editions, even with his manuscript alterations, away from his own 32-volume collected edition of his <u>Works</u>, issued 1771-4, back in nearly every case to the first edition, obviously the nearest to his manuscript. This, therefore, will usually form the basis of our presentation of his text. With it will be incorporated, however, all Wesley's major revisions of fact and of viewpoint, while all substantive changes of wording discovered in every edition which may have been revised by Wesley will be recorded in appendices. Thus we shall offer the general reader what we believe represents Wesley's most fully deliberate expression of his thought. At the same time, however, we shall enable the scholar to visualize the stages through which the text passed, and to evaluate personally the significance of every substantive variant reading from it. In fact, only a fraction of this definitive text will differ greatly from the traditional text. Nevertheless, the enormous undertaking is justified by the attempt to recover the freshness of Wesley's original thought, freed from the accretions of decades of error. There have also been compensatory gains (which could have been achieved in no other way), in gaining a fuller knowledge of Wesley's literary practices, and illuminating several aspects of his life, character, and thought. To a few examples of these we now turn.

Wesley's editors have constantly been plagued by the fact that he was always on the run. This was the chief complaint made against him by Dr. Samuel Johnson, who liked to get his feet stretched out for a long and leisurely conversation, but soon found Wesley looking at his watch and announcing that he had another appointment. [3] Similarly, Wesley wrote

on the run, and it was only during brief snatched intervals
that he was able to revise his writings. Even the character
of his original works was conditioned by his full pastoral
timetable. They were occasional, such as sermons and
tracts, or cumulative, like his Journal, rather than large
systematic works. His only major systematic works were
derivative from the writings of others. Publishing was an
extension of his preaching ministry, but he was rarely able
to give it his undivided attention for long.

As a result of this haste, numerous errors crept into
his manuscripts, and still more into his printed works, some
never to be removed. Nor were these merely slips in spell-
ing, in grammar, in syntax, which in any case must be
judged against the best practice of his own day rather than
that of ours, so that many phrases which ring uncomfortably
in our ears were euphonious at the time. He was also guilty,
however, of hardly ever checking his references, so that
thousands of quotations, from the Bible as well as from general and classical literature, are garbled, sometimes to the
extent of being almost unrecognizable. We find frequent errors of fact, over-hasty statements of opinion, and sentences
which are far from producing that plain and pointed English
for which he always strove and which he usually produced.
Two examples will suffice.

In his Explanatory Notes upon the New Testament,
writing of Christians who because they are God's elect should
therefore lead exemplary lives, he penned the sentence:
"Holiness is the consequence of their election, and God's superior love of their holiness." He apparently intended to say
that these Christians were holy because God had elected
them, and God had elected them because he was loving. The
first part he stated accurately enough--that God's election

led to men's holiness--but then went on to say in fact that
men's holiness in its turn led to God's superior love!
("Holiness is the consequence of their election, and God's superior love ['the consequence,' understood] of their holiness.")[4] He was in his early fifties when he wrote that sentence, which has never yet been corrected. Less under-
standable is a factual error made ten years earlier, which
again has gone uncorrected. In A Farther Appeal to Men
of Reason and Religion he claimed correctly that he had been
ordained deacon in 1725, but went on to state that his ordination as priest occurred one year later, instead of three.[5]
It must be admitted, however, that Wesley had a poor memory for dates, and often made mistakes in such relatively un-
important details.

Wesley's own manuscript errors, however, are infini-
tesimal compared with those of his printers. Even with the
best of printers errors are bound to occur, but Wesley was
occasionally served--or thwarted--by some of the worst. In
the fourth volume of his collected Sermons a lengthy passage
defining sin and Christian perfection was omitted from one is-
sue--the very issue which later he used as the basis for his
collected Works, though happily this passage was recovered
from the other issue and appears in later editions of his Sermons.[6] The Works themselves were very poorly printed,
and the errata sheets prepared for each of the 32 volumes--
but often not bound with them--deal with only the tip of the
iceberg. The printer even managed to omit one whole extract of Wesley's Journal, covering two years![7]

Unfortunately, the hurried efforts of Wesley or his appointed sub-editors to read the proofs frequently compounded
these errors with makeshift corrections which made superfi-
cial sense but hardly ever achieved the force of the original,

and occasionally obscured the whole point of a statement.   A
simple case is found in Wesley's sermon, "Of Evil Angels."
He wrote, "the very name of Satan, successor of Michael."
But it was January, 1783, and he was 79, and wrote in a
somewhat shaky hand, so that in setting up the text the com-
positor misread the word "successor" and introduced a new
being to the heavenly--or hellish--hierarchy: "the very name
of Satan, Lucess, or Michael." This was corrected back to
"Satan, successor of Michael" both in Wesley's personal copy
of The Arminian Magazine and in the printed errata issued
in 1786.   Yet when he collected his later sermons for publication in 1788, Wesley overlooked these errata, and made a
hasty guess, altering "Lucess" into something a little like it,
"Lucifer." This minimized the nonsense by supplying another
name for the evil angel Satan, but left both of them as syn-
onymous with the good angel, Michael.   Jackson's edition,
and therefore all subsequent texts, dutifully followed Wesley's
manifestly incorrect correction. [8]

A similar case involved not the misreading of a manuscript but the misplacement of a whole line of manuscript or
type by the printer.   In 1745, in A Farther Appeal to Men
of Reason and Religion, Wesley spoke of three things which
were necessary to justification: faith, which was "proximate-
ly necessary"; repentance, which was "remotely" necessary;
and "the fruits of repentance, still more remotely, as they
are necessary to repentance." The printer omitted the word
"faith" from the end of the second clause, and all but "repentance" which ended the third clause, so that the third
clause was in effect swallowed up in the second, to read,
"repentance, remotely, as it is necessary to the increase or
continuance of repentance." This was, of course, nonsense,
and in the following edition the closing word was replaced by

"faith." An errata slip had been prepared restoring the genuine text, but this was overlooked, so that all subsequent editions, including all editions of Wesley's <u>Works</u>, have omitted
one of the factors which Wesley claimed was necessary, even
though remotely, to true justification. [9]

With this background for the Wesley text it is not surprising that sometimes conjectural emendations are needed,
whether through the carelessness of Wesley himself, of his
printers, or a combination of both. In many instances a
word within brackets must be supplied to turn poor sense or
absolute nonsense into the good sense which Wesley apparently intended. In old age his handwriting was at times almost
illegible, and even those familiar with it had to guess, with
the aid of context, the identity of individual words. In the
case of his letters many of the errors which have crept into
Telford's edition can be corrected by comparison with other
extant letters from the same period. Where the original
manuscripts have disappeared, however, we cannot usually
travel beyond the realm of conjecture. In his last sermon,
completed January 17, 1791, Wesley wrote of the joys of
conversing in heaven with Adam, with Abraham, with Moses,
with David, the prophets, the apostles, the martyrs, the
saints, the angels. He continued (according to the editor and
printer of <u>The Arminian Magazine</u>), "Above all the name of
creature owns, with Jesus, the Mediator of the new covenant." The context, together with a similar passage in a
sermon of 1788, checked by a study of Wesley's handwriting
at the time, suggests that by the addition of one missing
word, "with," and readily acceptable changes in others, we
can supply a conjectural emendation which at least makes
sense: "Above all [with] the Lord of creation himself, with
Jesus, the mediator of the new covenant."[10]

Thus in many ways the careful study of the transmission of Wesley's text enables us to visualize his literary practices, and thus better to understand the text itself. In the process of this study, however, we also learn much about other aspects of his life, character, and thought. His skill in Greek is frequently underlined, as when in his Explanatory Notes he comes to 1 Cor. 10:12, where the Authorized version, which usually formed the basis of his own translation, reads, "Let him that thinketh he standeth take heed lest he fall." In the New English Bible this is transformed into the racy, "If you feel sure that you are standing firm, beware!" Wesley felt his way carefully to a less vigorous approximation to this kind of translation. At the proof stage he dropped the word "thinketh"; the passage then read, "Let him that standeth take heed lest he fall." Wesley pointed out in a note that in "the common translation ... the word translated 'thinketh' most certainly strengthens, rather than weakens, the sense. Perhaps it should be translated, 'he that most assuredly standeth.'" In the second edition he thus amended the translation itself, and dropped the note.[11]

The careful collation of the early editions reveals the fact that Wesley also had a sound working knowledge of Hebrew. He could trust himself to set down Hebrew words and phrases from memory, though his scholarship was not sufficiently detailed for him to be letter-perfect. Thus in the first edition of A Farther Appeal he spells ruach (spirit), with a central aleph instead of a waw,[12] and in his sermon, "The Way to the Kingdom," he quotes Ps. 32:1 as "blessed, or rather happy, is the man," adding to the Hebrew ha'ish (the man), which in fact was not present in the original text.[13] These minor errors, which must surely have been derived by the printer from Wesley's original manuscript,

were eventually corrected, but they are errors which demonstrate not only Wesley's unreadiness to check his references,
but also his familiarity with Hebrew and its limitations.

Another trait of his character revealed by this kind of
study is his uneasiness about a tendency to sarcasm, which
at times he deems it necessary to correct, whether for reasons of kindness or of prudence. In his Letter to the Lord
Bishop of London (1747), for instance, Wesley included comments which on cooler reflection seemed sufficiently indis-
creet for him to consider scrapping the whole edition, until
his brother Charles suggested striking out the passages by
hand and selling the pamphlet privately. One passage which
was thus struck through and disappeared from later editions
was the second part of a sentence in which Wesley challenged
Edmund Gibson--one of the most learned men of the day--"O
my lord, are these the words of a father of the Church, or
of a boy in the third class of Westminster School?"[14]

It is to Wesley's credit, however, that he was not
afraid to admit that he had been mistaken. Comparison of
the different editions brings to light many areas of thought in
which he changed his mind. In the first flush of enthusiasm
after his heart was "strangely warmed" on May 24, 1738, he
prepared the second extract from his Journal, in which he
spoke of himself as not having been a Christian, as having no
faith, until that day. Thirty years later he not only realized
that he had overstated the case, but that he ought to make
public confession of his error. The gist of what he tried to
say was this: "I certainly then had the faith of a servant,
though not the faith of a son." Unfortunately, by the time
that he had resolved to put this right in Vol. 26 of his collected Works, the volume was in print. Again unfortunately,
the errata sheet in which he made his corrections was issued

separately from the volume itself, so that the differing viewpoint was largely overlooked. He therefore tried a new tac-
tic. In 1775 he published a new 5th edition of the Journal
itself, with a new set of specially written footnotes pointing
out his changed views of his own spiritual condition in early
1738. This also was for the most part neglected by future
editors like Thomas Jackson and Nehemiah Curnock, so that
Wesley's eager but belated attempt to publicize his altered
viewpoint was almost totally lost. [15]

As we have seen, The Oxford Edition of Wesley's
Works is a project engaging in various capacities scholars
from several different nations and different denominations,
though the bulk of the key workers are Methodists from the
U.S.A. and England. The textual history of Wesley's writings emphasizes his own growing ecumenicity, as may be
seen in his attitude towards the Roman Catholic Church. In
the original edition of An Earnest Appeal to Men of Reason
and Religion Wesley strongly criticized that Church, but became confused in his dates, and therefore in quoting the can-
ons of the Council of Trent offered the opinion that "the very
design of the Council [was] ... to anathematize the Church of
England" for issuing its First Book of Homilies--which in
fact was issued later. When an opponent pointed out the error Wesley agreed that he had written hastily, "not having
the book by [him]." Thereupon he drastically revised the
erring section, but through lax control he was not successful
in preventing the original incorrect passage from appearing in
the majority of the remaining nine editions issued during his
lifetime. [16]

Wesley also tried to soften the impact of other statements written in the heat of emotion as well as in the grip
of strong prejudice against the Roman Catholic Church,

which mellowed as he grew older. Thus in his Journal for May 24, 1738, in the course of describing his spiritual pilgrimage up to that epochal day, he spoke of the unhappy influence upon him of the mystic writers, adding the comment, "who I declare in my cool judgment, and in the presence of of the Most High God, I believe to be one great Antichrist." In the 1765 and later editions he retained a reference to the effect of the mystics upon him, but omitted this stern early judgment, which is therefore not to be found in modern editions of his Works or of his Journal. Similarly, in his Sermon on Salvation by Faith, 1738, he spoke about "all the errors of that apostate Church," but his collected Sermons (first published 1746) omitted the word "apostate," though he took no pains to expunge the harsh epithet from the many separate editions of the sermon which continued to appear.

Such was Wesley's basic honesty, as well as his burning passion for God, that we believe he would be happy to know that at long last we shall be able to read and understand more fully the writings in which he revealed himself to the world as he proclaimed the gospel, and to see him warts and all!

NOTES

1. Methodist History, Vol. VIII, Number 4 (July, 1970), pp. 48-8; Duke Divinity School Review, XXXVI, pp. 87-99 (Spring, 1971); The Methodist Churchman, Vol. 15, No. 3 (May, 1972).

2. The Doctrine of Original Sin, owned by Prof. Albert C. Outler, and Explanatory Notes upon the New Testament, owned by Mrs. E. P. Prothro, and deposited in Bridwell Library, Perkins School of Theology, Dallas.

3. James Boswell, Boswell's Life of Samuel Johnson, ed-
    ited by George B. Hill (New York: Harper & Brothers,
    1889), Vol. III, p. 261.

4. In this instance we suggest the conjectural emendation,
    "God's superior love [the cause] of their [election],"
    with a footnote ["original, election"].

5. A Farther Appeal, Part I, VI. 1, p. 176 of Vol. 11,
    new edition.

6. Sermons, Vol. IV, 1760, including "Thoughts on Chris-
    tian Perfection," pp. 237-67, in the issue by John
    Grabham, of Bristol, which contains 36 questions; and
    pp. 237-68 in that by John Grabham and William Pine,
    which contains 38.

7. Works, Vol. 29, 1774, which omitted Journal VIII, part-
    ly through misnumbering, moving from July 20, 1749
    straight to November 2, 1751.

8. See Arminian Magazine, VI, p. 120 (March, 1783); cf.
    Sermons (1788), VI, p. 129, and Works, ed. Thomas
    Jackson, VI, p. 372.

9. See new edition, Vol. 11, p. 117; the omission is con-
    tinued in Wesley's letter to Horne, ibid, p. 451.
    Similarly, in the Explanatory Notes the printer of the
    2nd edition dropped a line of type in Gal. 3:22n, which
    happened to be a complete parenthesis describing his
    intention of the clause, "the Scripture hath concluded
    all under sin": "(not only all men, but all they have,
    do, and are)." This was never recovered.

10. The Arminian Magazine, XIV, p. 402 (August, 1791);
    cf. Works, ed. T. Jackson, VII, pp. 234, 331-2.
    For another conjectural emendation see note 4 above.

11. Wesley similarly anticipated modern translations in a
    host of other instances such as Matt. 6:22, "The eye
    is the lamp of the body," and Matt. 13:25, "the enemy
    came and sowed tares," amended at the proof stage
    to "darnel."

12. Part I, I.6, p. 108; cf. III.5 and note, p. 125.

13. "The Way to the Kingdom" I:11; cf. Works, ed. Jack-

son, V, p. 80, though he omits Wesley's original Hebrew.

14. A Letter to the Lord Bishop of London, par. 6, 11, pp.
338, 343 of new edition.

15. Frank Baker, "Aldersgate and Wesley's Editors," London Quarterly Review, Vol. 191, pp. 310-19 (Oct.
1966). Cf. Explanatory Notes, John 9:16, "How can
a man that is a sinner do such miracles?" To this
the first two editions of 1755 and 1757 append the
note, "a man that is a sinner, that is, such a sinner
as to be incapable of being sent by God"; in 1760 this
was softened to the note which became traditional, "a
sinner, that is, one living in wilful sin."

16. par. 58; see new edition, pp. 68-9.

THE PLACE OF JOHN WESLEY
IN THE CHRISTIAN TRADITION

A SELECTED BIBLIOGRAPHY

Lawrence D. McIntosh

This bibliography was compiled in the interests of the Consultation in celebration of the Commencement of the publication of the Oxford Edition of the Works of John Wesley, held at Drew University, Madison, New Jersey on October 9-11, 1974.

CONTENTS

           a. Eighteenth century
           b. Nineteenth century
           c. Twentieth century
      iv. John Wesley and his Contemporaries
       v. Doctrine and Practice
           a. Wesley's Theology: comprehensive
           b. The word and work of God
           c. The meaning of Salvation
           d. Churchmanship
           e. The Sacraments
           f. Preaching
           g. Pastoral Care
           h. Social Concerns
           i. Readings and Publishing
           j. Ecumenical Trends

III. EIGHTEENTH CENTURY BRITISH METHODISM

I. THE EIGHTEENTH CENTURY

A. Eighteenth century background

Becker, C. L. The Heavenly City of the Eighteenth Century
    Philosophers. New Haven: Yale Univ. Pr., 1932.

Bethell, S. L. The Cultural Revolution of the Seventeenth
    Century. London: Dobson, 1951.

Butterfield, Herbert. "England in the Eighteenth Century."
    In A History of the Methodist Church in Great Britain
    pp. 1-33. Edited by Rupert Davies and E. Gordon
    Rupp. London: Epworth Pr., 1965.

Clifford, James L., ed. Man versus Society in Eighteenth-
    Century Britain: Six Points of View. Cambridge Univ.
    Pr., 1968.

Cragg, G. R. Reason and Authority in the Eighteenth Cen-
    tury. Cambridge Univ. Pr., 1964.

Hunt, John. Religious Thought in England. 3 vols. Lon-
    don: Strahan, 1870-1873.

Lovejoy, Arthur O.   The Great Chain of Being: A Study in
    the History of an Idea.   New York: Harper, 1960.

Merton, R. K.   "Science, Technology and Society in Seven-
    teenth Century England."   Osiris 4 (1938): 360-632.

Plumb, J. H.   England in the Eighteenth Century.   Harmonds-
    worth: Penguin, 1952.

Robbins, Caroline.   The Eighteenth-Century Commonwealth-
    man: Studies in the Transmission, Development and
    Circumstance of English Liberal Thought from the Res-
    toration of Charles II until the War with the Thirteen
    Colonies.   Cambridge, Mass.:   Harvard Univ. Pr., 1961.

Rupp, Gordon.   Six Makers of English Religion, 1500-1700.
    London: Hodder and Stoughton, 1957.

Stephen, Leslie.   History of English Thought in the Eigh-
    teenth Century.   3rd ed. 2 vols.   New York: G. P.
    Putnam's Sons, 1902.

Stromberg, Roland N.   Religious Liberalism in Eighteenth
    Century England.   Oxford Univ. Pr., 1954.

Tulloch, John.   Rational Theology and Christian Philosophy
    in England in the Seventeenth Century.   2 vols.   Edin-
    burgh: Blackwood, 1874.

Walker, Daniel Pickering.   The Ancient Theology: Studies
    in Christian Platonism from the Fifteenth to the Eigh-
    teenth Century.   Ithaca: Cornell Univ. Pr., 1972.

Westfall, R. S.   Science and Religion in Seventeenth-Century
    England.   New Haven: Yale Univ. Pr., 1958.

Whitely, J. H.   Wesley's England: a Survey of Eighteenth
    Century Social and Cultural Conditions.   London: Ep-
    worth Pr., 1938.

Willey, Basil.   The Eighteenth Century Background.   Boston:
    Beacon, 1961.

B. The Church in England

   i. General

Knox, R. Buick. "The Appeal to Antiquity." The Expository
   Times 80, 10 (July 1969) 297-301.

Moorman, John R. H. A History of the Church of England.
   3rd ed. London: Black, 1973.

Neill, Stephen. Anglicanism. Harmondsworth: Penguin,
   1958.

Sykes, Norman. The English Religious Tradition. London:
   S. C. M. , 1953.

   ii. The Church in the 17th and 18th centuries

Abbey, Charles J. and Overton, John H. The English Church
   in the Eighteenth Century. 2 vols. London: Longmans
   Green, 1878.

Carpenter, S. C. Eighteenth Century Church and People.
   London: Murray, 1959.

Chadwick, William Owen. "Arminianism in England." Religion in Life 29 (1960) 548-555.

Cragg, G. R. , ed. The Cambridge Platonists. Oxford Univ.
   Pr., 1968.

_____. The Church and the Age of Reason, 1648-1789.
   Harmondsworth: Penguin, 1960.

_____. From Puritanism to the Age of Reason. Cam-
   bridge Univ. Pr. , 1950.

Crane, R. S. "Anglican Apologetics and the Idea of Progress,
   1699-1745." Modern Philology 31 (1934) 273-306; 349-
   382.

Creed, J. M. and Boys Smith, J. S. Religious Thought in
   the Eighteenth Century. Cambridge Univ. Pr. , 1934.

Davies, Horton. Worship and Theology in England: From
   Watts and Wesley to Maurice, 1690-1850. Princeton

Univ. Pr., 1961.

Knox, R. A. Enthusiasm: A Chapter in the History of Re-
    ligion with Special Reference to the XVII and XVIII Cen-
    turies. Oxford: Clarendon Pr., 1950.

McAdoo, H. R. The Spirit of Anglicanism. New York:
    Scribners, 1965.

_____. The Structure of Caroline Moral Theology. Lon-
    don: Longmans, 1949.

More, P. E., and Cross, F. L. Anglicanism. London:
    S. P. C. K., 1935.

Nuttall, Geoffrey. "The Influence of Arminianism in Eng-
    land." In his The Puritan Spirit, pp. 67-80. London:
    Epworth Pr., 1967.

Parker, T. M. "Arminianism and Laudianism in Seventeenth
    Century England." In Studies in Church History. Vol.
    1, pp. 20-34. Edited by C. W. Dugmore and C. Duggen.
    London: Nelson, 1964.

Stoeffler, F. Ernest. The Rise of Evangelical Pietism.
    Leiden: Brill, 1965.

Sykes, Norman. Church and State in England in the XVIIIth
    Century. Cambridge Univ. Pr., 1934.

_____. From Sheldon to Secker. Cambridge Univ. Pr.,
    1959.

_____. William Wake, Archbishop of Canterbury, 1657-
    1737. 2 vols. Cambridge Univ. Pr., 1957.

Trevor-Roper, Hugh. The Crisis of the Seventeenth Century:
    Religion, the Reformation and Social Change. New York:
    Harper and Row, 1968.

Wood, A. Skevington. The Inextinguishable Blaze: Spiritual
    Renewal and Advance in the Eighteenth Century. London:
    Paternoster Pr., 1960.

II. JOHN WESLEY, HIS LIFE AND THOUGHT

A. Primary Sources:

i. Bibliographies

Baker, Frank, ed. A Union Catalogue of the Publications of John Charles Wesley. Durham, North Carolina: The Divinity School, Duke University, 1966.

Green, Richard. The Works of John and Charles Wesley: A Bibliography. London: Kelly, 1896.

ii. Writings of John Wesley

The Arminian Magazine: Consisting of Extracts and Original Treatises on Universal Redemption, ed. John Wesley. London: Fry et al, 1778-1791-.

A Christian Library: Consisting of Extracts from, and Abridgments of, the Choicest Pieces of Practical Divinity Which Have Been Published in the English Tongue. 50 vols. Bristol: Farley, 1749-1755.

Explanatory Notes upon the New Testament. 3 vols. 3rd ed. Bristol: Grabham and Pine, 1760-1762.

John Wesley's Letter to a Roman Catholic. Edited by Michael Hurley, S.J. London: Geoffrey Chapman, 1968.

The Journal of the Rev. John Wesley, A.M. Edited by Nehemiah Curnock. 8 vols. London: Epworth Pr., 1909-1916.

The Letters of the Rev. John Wesley, A.M. Edited by John Telford. 8 vols. London: Epworth Pr., 1931.

Wesley's Standard Sermons. Edited by E. H. Sugden. 2 vols. London: Epworth Pr., 1921.

The Works of the Rev. John Wesley, M.A. 32 vols. Bristol: Pine, 1771-1774.

The Works of the Rev. John Wesley, M.A. Edited by Thomas Jackson. 14 vols. London: Mason, 1829-1831.

(Baker, Frank. "The Oxford Edition of Wesley's Works."
   Methodist History 8, 4 (July 1970), 41-48.)

   iii. Selections

Burtner, R. W., and Chiles, R. E., eds. A Compend of
   Wesley's Theology. New York: Abingdon, 1954.

Outler, Albert C., ed. John Wesley. New York: Oxford
   Univ. Pr., 1964.

Watson, Philip. The Message of the Wesleys. New York:
   Macmillan, 1964.

B. Secondary Sources

   i. Bibliographies

Bowmer, John C. "Twenty-Five Years (1943-1968): I. The
   Work of the Wesley Historical Society; II. Methodist
   Studies." Proc. Wesley Historical Society 37 (1969) 33-
   36; 61-66.

Judson, Sandra. Biographical and Descriptive Works on the
   Rev. John Wesley. London: University of London, 1963.

Melton, J. Gordon. "An Annotated Bibliography of Publications about the Life and Work of John Wesley, 1791-
   1966." Methodist History 7, 4 (July 1969) 29-46.

Norwood, Frederick A. "Methodist Historical Studies, 1930-
   1959." Church History 28 (1959) 391-417; 29 (1960) 74-
   88.

_____. "Wesleyan and Methodist Historical Studies, 1960-
   1970: A Bibliographical Article." Church History 40
   (1971) 182-199.

Rogal, Samuel J. "The Wesleys: A Checklist of Critical
   Commentary." Bulletin of Bibliography and Magazine
   Notes 28, 1 (January-March 1971), 22-35.

   Dissertations

"Academic Theses on Methodist History." Proc. Wesley

Historical Society 34 (1963) 52; 99; 35 (1965-1966) 55,
136; 36 (1967) 91; 37 (1970) 196; 38 (1971) 95.

Hardman, Keith J.   "Checklist of Doctoral Dissertations on
    Methodist, Evangelical United Brethren, and Related Sub-
    jects, 1912-1968." Methodist History 8, 3 (April 1970)
    38-42.

    Continued by the Editors as:

"Supplementary Checklist of Doctoral Dissertations on Meth-
    odist and Related Subjects." Methodist History 9, 3 (Ap-
    pril 1971), 63-61; 10, 3 (April 1972) 59-60; 11, 3 (April
    1973) 52-53; 12, 3 (April 1974), 57-59.

    ii.   The Wesley Family

Baker, Frank.   Charles Wesley: As Revealed by His Letters.
    London: Epworth Pr. , 1948.

_____ .   Charles Wesley's Verse: An Introduction.   Lon-
    don: Epworth Pr. , 1964.

_____ .   Representative Verse of Charles Wesley.   London:
    Epworth Pr. , 1962.

_____ .   "Salute to Susanna." Methodist History 7, 3 (Ap-
    ril 1969) 3-12.

Clarke, Adam.   Memoirs of the Wesley Family.   4th ed.   2
    vols. London: Tegg, 1866.

Edwards, Maldwyn.   Family Circle: A Study of the Epworth
    Household in Relation to John and Charles Wesley.   Lon-
    don: Epworth Pr. , 1949.

Gill, Frederick Cyril.   Charles Wesley, the First Methodist.
    New York: Abingdon, 1965.

Jackson, Thomas.   Life of the Rev. Charles Wesley.   2 vols.
    London: Mason, 1841.

Newton, John A.   "Susanna Wesley (1669-1742): A Biblio-
    graphical Survey." Proc. Wesley Historical Society 37
    (June 1969) 37-40.

_____. Susanna Wesley and the Puritan Tradition in Methodism.   London: Epworth Pr. , 1968.

Rattenbury, J. Ernest.   The Evangelical Doctrines of Charles Wesley's Hymns.   London: Epworth Pr. , 1941.

Stevenson, George.   Memorials of the Wesley Family.   London: Partridge, 1876.

Tyerman, Luke.   Life and Times of Samuel Wesley.   London: Simpkin and Marshall, 1866.

Wesley, Charles.   Journal.   Edited by Thomas Jackson.   2 vols.   London: Wesleyan Methodist Book Room, [1881?].

iii. Biographical Studies

Eighteenth Century

(Maser, Frederick.   "The Early Biographers of John Wesley."   Methodist History 1, 2 (January 1963) 29-42.)

Coke, Thomas and Moore, Henry.   The Life of the Rev. John Wesley, A. M.   London: Paramora, 1792.

Hampson, John.   Memoirs of the late Rev. John Wesley, A. M.   3 vols.   Sunderland: Graham, 1791.

"Obituary. "   Gentleman's Magazine 61 (March 1791) 282-284.

Whitehead, John.   The Life of the Rev. John Wesley, A. M. 2 vols.   London: Couchman, 1793, 1796.

Nineteenth Century

Hockin, Frederick.   John Wesley and Modern Methodism. 4th ed.   London: Rivington, 1887.

Holden, H. W.   John Wesley in Company with High Churchmen.   4th ed.   London: Hodges, 1871.

Moors, Henry.   The Life of the Rev. John Wesley, A. M. 2 vols.   London: Kershaw, 1824-1825.

Overton, J. H.   John Wesley.   London: Methuen, 1891.

Southey, Robert. The Life of Wesley and the Rise and Prog-
    ress of Methodism. 2 vols. 3rd ed. London: Long-
    mans, 1846.

Tyerman, Luke. The Life and Times of the Rev. John Wes-
    ley, M.A. 3 vols. London: Hodder and Stoughton,
    1870-1871.

Urlin, R. Denny. The Churchman's Life of Wesley. Lon-
    don: S.P.C.K., 1880.

_____. John Wesley's Place in Church History. London:
    Rivington, 1870.

Watson, Richard. The Life of the Rev. John Wesley, A.M.
    London: Mason, 1831.

Twentieth Century

Andrews, Stuart. "John Wesley and the Age of Reason."
    History Today 19 (January 1969) 25-32.

Baker, Frank. "'Aldersgate' and Wesley's Editors." Lon-
    don Quarterly and Holborn Review 191 (1966) 310-319.

_____. "Aldersgate 1738-1963: The Challenge of Alders-
    gate." Duke Divinity School Bulletin 28, 2 (May 1963)
    67-80.

_____. "The Birth of John Wesley's Journal." Methodist
    History 8, 2 (January 1970) 25-32.

_____. "John Wesley's First Marriage." London Quarter-
    ly and Holborn Review 192 (1967) 305-315.

_____. "The Real John Wesley." Methodist History 12,
    4 (July 1974) 183-197.

_____. "Wesley's Puritan Ancestry." London Quarterly
    and Holborn Review 187 (1962) 180-186.

Borgen, Ole E. John Wesley: An Autobiographical Sketch of
    the Man and His Thought, Chiefly from His Letters.
    Guilford: Conn.: Albert Brill, 1966.

Cannon, William R. "John Wesley's Years in Georgia."
    Methodist History N.S. 1, 4 (July 1963) 1-7.

Edwards, Maldwyn. The Astonishing Youth. London: Ep-
    worth Pr. , 1959.

Fitchett, W. H. Wesley and His Century. New York: Eat-
    on and Mains, 1906.

Gill, F. C. In the Steps of John Wesley. London: Lutter-
    worth Pr. , 1962.

Green, V. H. H. John Wesley. London: Nelson, 1964.

_____. The Young Mr. Wesley: A Study of John Wesley
    and Oxford. London: Arnold, 1961.

Harrison, G. Elsie. Son to Susanna: The Private Life of
    John Wesley. London: Nicholson and Watson, 1937.

Heitzenrater, Richard. "John Wesley and the Oxford Method-
    ists, 1725-1735." Ph. D. dissertation. Duke University,
    1972.

_____. "The Oxford Diaries and the First Rise of Meth-
    odism." Methodist History 12, 4 (July 1974) 110-135.

Holland, Bernard G. "The Conversions of John and Charles
    Wesley and Their Place in Methodist Tradition. " Proc.
    Wesley Historical Society 38 (1971) 46-53; 65-71.

Leger, J. A. John Wesley's Last Love. London: Dent,
    1910.

McIntosh, Lawrence D. "John Wesley: Conversion as a
    Continuum. " Mid-Stream 8, 3 (Spring 1969) 50-65.

McNeill, John T. "Luther at Aldersgate." London Quarter-
    ly and Holborn Review 164 (April 1939) 200-217.

Randolph, J. Ralph. "John Wesley and the American Indian:
    A Study in Disillusionment. " Methodist History 10, 3
    (April 1972), 3-11.

Rattenbury, J. Ernest. The Conversion of the Wesleys.
    London: Epworth Pr. , 1938.

Schmidt, Martin. John Wesley: A Theological Biography.
    2 vols. in 3 pts. New York: Abingdon, 1962 (1963),
    1972, 1973. Vol. I: From 17th June until 24th May

1738; Vol. 2: Pts. I and II: John Wesley's Life Mission.

_____. "John Wesley als Organisator der methodistischen Bewegung." In Für Kirche und Recht: Festschrift für J. Heckel, pp. 313-350. Cologne: Böhlau Verlag, 1959.

_____. The Young Wesley: Missionary and Theologian of Missions. London: Epworth Pr., 1958. (trans. of Der Junge Wesley als Heidenmissioner und Missionstheologe. Gutersloh, 1955; 2nd ed. 1974).

Simon, J. S. John Wesley and the Religious Societies. London: Epworth Pr., 1921.

_____. John Wesley and the Methodist Societies. London: Epworth Pr., 1923.

_____. John Wesley and the Advance of Methodism. London: Epworth Pr., 1925.

_____. John Wesley, the Master Builder. London: Epworth Pr., 1927.

_____. John Wesley, the Last Phase. London: Epworth Pr., 1934.

Telford, John. The Life of John Wesley. 3rd ed. London: Kelly, 1910.

Wood, A. Skevington. The Burning Heart: John Wesley, Evangelist. Exeter: Paternoster Pr., 1967.

iv.   John Wesley and his Contemporaries

Baker, Eric W. A Herald of the Evangelical Revival: A Critical Inquiry into the Relation of William Law to John Wesley and the Beginnings of Methodism. London: Epworth Pr., 1948.

_____. "Whitefield's Break with the Wesleys." The Church Quarterly 3, 2 (October 1970), 103-113.

_____. William Grimshaw, 1708-1763. London: Epworth Pr., 1963.

Brown, Earl Kent. "Standing in the Shadow: Women in Early Methodism." Nexus 17, 2 (Spring 1974) 22-31.

Dallimore, Arnold. George Whitefield, Vol. I. London: Banner of Truth Trust, 1970.

Edwards, Maldwyn. "Adam Clarke: The Man." Methodist History 9, 4 (July 1971) 50-56.

_____. "Two Master Builders: The Relation of John Wesley and Francis Asbury." Proc. Wesley Historical Society 38, 2 (August 1971), 42-45.

English, John C. "John Norris and John Wesley on the 'Conduct of the Understanding'." Proc. Wesley Historical Society 37 (February 1970) 101-104.

Godbold, Albea. "Francis Asbury and his Difficulties with John Wesley and Thomas Rankin." Methodist History 3, 3 (April 1965) 3-19.

Green, Richard B. Anti-Methodist Publications Issued during the Eighteenth Century. London: Kelly, 1902.

Green, William. John Wesley and William Law. London: Epworth Pr., 1945.

Knox, Alexander. Remains. 4 vols. 3rd ed. London: Duncan and Malcolm, 1844.

Knox, R. B. "The Wesleys and Howell Harris." Studies in Church History, vol. 3, pp. 267-276. Edited by G. J. Cumming. Leiden: Brill, 1966.

Lang, Edward. Francis Asbury's Reading of Theology: A Bibliographic Study. Evanston: Garrett Theological Seminary Library, 1972.

Maycock, J. "The Fletcher-Toplady Controversy." London Quarterly and Holborn Review 191 (1966) 227-235.

Mitchell, David. "Queen of the Methodists: Selina, Countess of Huntingdon." History Today 15, 12 (December 1965) 846-854.

The Oxford Methodists. London: Roberts, 1733.

Priestley, Joseph ed. Original Letters by the Rev. John Wesley and His Friends, Illustrative of His Early History. Birmingham: Pearson, 1791.

(Seymour, A. C. H.). The Life and Times of Selina, Countess of Huntingdon. 2 vols. London: Painter, 1840.

Shipley, David C. "Methodist Arminianism in the Theology of John Fletcher." Ph.D. dissertation, Yale University, 1942.

Snow, M. Lawrence. "Methodist Enthusiasm: Warburton Letters, 1738-1740." Methodist History 10, 2 (April 1972) 30-47.

Stein, Stephen J. "George Whitefield on Slavery: Some New Evidence." Church History 42, 2 (June 1973), 243-256.

Towlson, Clifford W. Moravian and Methodist. London: Epworth Pr., 1957.

Tyerman, Luke. The Life of the Reverend George Whitefield. 2 vols. New York: Randolph, 1877.

_____. The Oxford Methodists. London: Hodder and Stoughton, 1873.

_____. Wesley's Designated Successor: The Life, Letters and Literary Labours of the Rev. John William Fletcher. London: Hodder and Stoughton, 1882.

Vickers, John A. "Coke and Asbury: A Comparison of Bishops." Methodist History 11, 1 (October 1972) 42-51.

_____. Thomas Coke: Apostle of Methodism. New York: Abingdon, 1969.

Walker, A. Keith. William Law: His Life and Thought. London: S. P. C. K., 1973.

Wiggins, James. The Embattled Saint: Aspects of the Life and Thought of John Fletcher. (Wesleyan Studies No. 2.) Macon, Georgia: Wesleyan College, 1966.

v.   Doctrine and Practice

a. Wesley's Theology: comprehensive

Arnett, William.   "John Wesley: Man of One Book."   Ph. D.
dissertation, Drew University, 1954.

Blankenship, Paul F.   "The Significance of John Wesley's
Abridgment of the Thirty-Nine Articles as Seen from
His Deletions."   Methodist History 2, 3 (April 1964) 35-
47.

Cannon, William R.   "Methodism in a Philosophy of History."
Methodist History 12, 4 (July 1974) 27-43.

_____.   The Theology of John Wesley, with Special Ref-
erence to the Doctrine of Justification.   New York: Abingdon, 1946.

Cell, George Croft.   The Rediscovery of John Wesley.   New
York, Henry Holt, 1935.

Chandler, Douglas R.   "John Wesley and the Uses of the
Past."   In Foundations of Theological Education; The
1972 Willson Lectures, pp. 27-37.   Washington, D. C. :
Wesley Theological Seminary, (1972).

Cushman, Robert E.   "Theological Landmarks in the Revival
under Wesley."   Religion in Life 27 (1957-1958) 105-118.

Eayrs, George.   John Wesley, Christian Philosopher and
Church Founder.   London: Epworth, 1926.

Edwards, Clifford W. , ed.   Japanese Contributions to the
Study of John Wesley.   (Wesleyan Studies No. 3).   Macon, Georgia: Wesleyan College, 1967.

English, John C.   "John Wesley and the Anglican Moderates
of the Seventeenth Century."   Anglican Theological Review 51, 3 (July 1969) 203-220.

Faulkner, John Alfred.   Wesley as Sociologist, Theologian,
Churchman.   New York: Methodist Book Concern, 1918.

Hildebrandt, Franz.   Christianity According to the Wesleys.
London: Epworth Pr. , 1955.

_____. From Luther to Wesley. London: Lutterworth, 1951.

Knight, John Allan. "Aspects of Wesley's Theology after 1770." Methodist History 6, 3 (April 1968), 33-42.

Lee, Umphrey. John Wesley and Modern Religion. Nashville: Cokesbury Pr., 1936.

Lerch, David. Heil und Heiligung bei John Wesley. Zurich: Christliche Vereinsbuchhandlung, 1941.

McIntosh, Lawrence D. "The Nature and Design of Christianity in John Wesley's Early Theology: A Study in the Relationship of Love and Faith." Ph. D. dissertation, Drew University 1966.

Meredith, Lawrence. "Essential Doctrine in the Theology of John Wesley: With Special Attention to Methodist Standards of Doctrine." Ph. D. dissertation, Harvard University 1962.

Michalson Carl. "The Hermeneutics of Holiness in Wesley." In The Heritage of Christian Thought: Essays in Honor of Robert Lowry Calhoun, pp. 127-141. Edited by Robert E. Cushman and Egil Grislis. New York: Harper and Row, 1965.

Monk, Robert C. John Wesley: His Puritan Heritage. New York: Abingdon, 1966.

Newton, John A. Methodism and the Puritans. London: Dr. Williams's Trust, 1964.

Orcibal, Jean. "Le Spirituals Français et Espagnols chez John Wesley et ses Contemporains." Revue de l'Histoire des Religions 139 (1951) 50-109.

Outler, Albert C. "John Wesley as Theologian--Then and Now." Methodist History 12, 4 (July 1974), 63-82.

_____. "Methodism's Theological Heritage: A Study in Perspective." In Methodism's Destiny in the Ecumenical Age, pp. 44-70. Edited by Paul M. Minus. New York: Abingdon, 1969.

_____. "Towards a Re-appraisal of John Wesley as a

Theologian. " Perkins Journal 14, 2 (Winter 1961) 5-14.

Piette, Maximin. John Wesley in the Evolution of Protestantism. New York: Sheed and Ward, 1937.

Sanders, Paul. "The Puritans and John Wesley." Work/
Worship 17, 2 (1967) 13-19.

Williams, Colin W. John Wesley's Theology Today. New
York: Abingdon, 1960.

        b.   The word and work of God

Deschner, John. Wesley's Christology: An Interpretation.
Dallas: Southern Methodist Univ. Pr., 1960.

Frost, Stanley B. Die Autoritatslehre in den Werken John
Wesley. Münich: Reinhardt, 1938.

Hildebrandt, Franz. "Wesley's Christology." Proc. Wesley
Historical Society 33 (June 1962) 122-124.

Starkey, Lycurgus M. The Work of the Holy Spirit: A Study
in Wesleyan Theology. New York: Abingdon, 1962.

Wilson, D. Dunn. "John Wesley's Break with Mysticism Re-
considered." Proc. Wesley Historical Society 3, 5 (September 1965) 65-67.

        c.   The meaning of Salvation

Cannon, William R. "John Wesley's Doctrine of Sanctification and Perfection." Mennonite Quarterly Review 35
(1961) 91-95.

_____. "Salvation in the Theology of John Wesley."
Methodist History 9 1 (October 1970) 3-12.

Cushman, Robert E. "Salvation for All: Wesley and Calvinism." In Methodism pp. 103-115. Edited by William
K. Anderson. Nashville: Methodist Publishing House,
1947.

English, John C. The Heart Renewed: John Wesley's Doctrine of Christian Initiation. (Wesleyan Studies No. 4).
Macon, Georgia: Wesleyan College, 1967.

Flew, R. Newton. The Idea of Perfection in Christian The-
    ology. Oxford Univ. Pr., 1934.

Hall, Thor. "The Christian's Life: Wesley's Alternative to
    Luther and Calvin." Duke Divinity School Bulletin 28,
    2 (May 1963) 111-126.

Hoon, Paul W. "The Soteriology of John Wesley." Ph.D.
    dissertation, Edinburgh University 1936.

Howe, Leroy T. "Some Wesleyan Thoughts on the Grace of
    God." Perkins Journal 25, 1 (Fall 1971) 19-28.

Koerber, Charles J. The Theology of Conversion According
    to John Wesley. New York: By the Author, 1967.

Lindström, Harald. Wesley and Sanctification. London:
    Epworth Pr., 1950.

Newton, John A. "Perfection and Spirituality in the Method-
    ist Tradition." The Church Quarterly 3, 2 (October
    1970) 95-103.

Rogers, Charles A. "The Concept of Prevenient Grace in
    the Theology of John Wesley." Ph.D. dissertation,
    Duke University, 1967.

Sangster, W. E. The Path to Perfection. New York: Ab-
    ingdon, 1943.

Schempp, Johannes. Seelsorge und Seelenführung bei John
    Wesley. Stuttgart: Christliches Verlagshaus, 1949.

Shipley, David C. "Wesley and Some Calvinistic Contro-
    versies." The Drew Gateway 25 (Summer 1955) 195-210.

Smith, Harmon L. "Wesley's Doctrine of Justification: Be-
    ginning and Process." Duke Divinity School Bulletin 28,
    2 (May 1963), 88-98.

Smith, J. Waldon. "Some Notes on Wesley's Doctrine of
    Prevenient Grace." Religion in Life 34 (Winter 1964-
    1965) 68-80.

Stoeffler, F. Ernest. "The Wesleyan Concept of Religious
    Certainty." London Quarterly and Holborn Review 189
    (1964) 128-138.

Walters, Orville S.   "The Concept of Attainment in John
    Wesley's Christian Perfection." Methodist History 10, 3
    (April 1972) 12-29.

_____. "John Wesley's Footnotes to Christian Perfec-
    tion." Methodist History 12, 1 (October 1973), 19-36.

Watson, Philip S.   "Wesley and Luther on Christian Perfec-
    tion." Ecumenical Review 15 (April 1963) 291-302.

Weissbach, Jürgen. Der neue Mensch in theologischen
    Denken John Wesleys. Stuttgart: Christliches Verlags-
    haus, 1970.

Yates, Arthur S. The Doctrine of Assurance with Special
    Reference to John Wesley. London: Epworth Pr., 1952.

          d.   Churchmanship

Baker, Frank. John Wesley and the Church of England. Lon-
    don: Epworth Pr.; New York: Abingdon, 1970.

_____. "John Wesley's Churchmanship." London Quarter-
    ly and Holborn Review 185 (1960) 210-215; 269-274.

Bowmer, John C.   "The Wesleyan Conception of the Minis-
    try." Religion in Life 40, 1 (Spring 1971) 85-96.

Cannon, William R.   "The Meaning of the Ministry in Meth-
    odism." Methodist History 8, 1 (October 1969) 3-19.

Dearing, Trevor. Wesleyan and Tractarian Worship. Lon-
    don: Epworth Pr.; S.P.C.K., 1966.

Durbin, Linda M.   "The Nature of Ordination in Wesley's
    View of the Ministry." Methodist History 9, 3 (April
    1971) 3-20.

English, John C.   "John Wesley and the Principle of Minis-
    terial Succession." Methodist History 2, 2 (January
    1964) 31-36.

Hofler, Durward.   "The Methodist Doctrine of the Church."
    Methodist History 6, 1 (October 1967) 25-35.

Kent, John H. S.   "John Wesley's Churchmanship." Proc.
    Wesley Historical Society 35 (1965) 10-14.

Lawson, A. B.   John Wesley and the Christian Ministry.
    London: S. P. C. K., 1963.

Outler, Albert C.   "Do Methodists Have a Doctrine of the
    Church?"   In The Doctrine of the Church, pp. 11-28.
    Edited by Dow Kirkpatrick.   New York: Abingdon Pr.,
    1964.

Rigg, James H.   The Relations of John Wesley and of Wes-
    leyan Methodism to the Church of England Investigated
    and Determined.   2nd ed.   London: Longmans, 1871.

Thompson, Edgar W.   Wesley: Apostolic Man: Some Re-
    flections on Wesley's Consecration of Dr. Thomas Coke.
    London: Epworth Pr., 1957.

                    e.   The Sacraments

Borgen, Ole E.   John Wesley on the Sacraments: A Theo-
    logical Study.   New York: Abingdon Pr., 1972.

Bowmer, John C.   The Sacrament of the Lord's Supper in
    Early Methodism.   London: Dacre, 1951.

English, John C.   "The Sacrament of Baptism According to
    the Sunday Service of 1784."   Methodist History 5, 2
    (January 1967) 10-16.

George, A. Raymond.   "The Lord's Supper."   In The Doc-
    trine of the Church, pp. 140-160.   Edited by Dow Kirk-
    patrick.   New York: Abingdon, 1964.

_____.   "The Real Presence and the Lord's Supper."
    Proc. Wesley Historical Society 34, 8 (December 1964)
    181-187.

Grislis, Egil.   "The Wesleyan Doctrine of the Lord's Sup-
    per."   Duke Divinity School Bulletin 28, 2 (May 1963)
    99-110.

Hildebrandt, Franz.   I Offered Christ: A Protestant Study
    of the Mass.   London: Epworth Pr., 1967.

Holland, Bernard.   Baptism in Early Methodism.   London:
    Epworth Pr., 1970.

Parris, John.   John Wesley's Doctrine of the Sacraments.

London: Epworth Pr., 1963.

Rattenbury, J. Ernest. The Eucharistic Hymns of John and
   Charles Wesley. London: Epworth Pr., 1948.

Sanders, Paul S. "An Appraisal of John Wesley's Sacramen-
   talism in the Evolution of Early American Methodism."
   Ph. D. dissertation, Union Theological Seminary, New
   York, 1954.

_____. "Wesley's Eucharistic Faith and Practice." Ang-
   lican Theological Review 148, 2 (April 1966) 157-174.

         f.   Preaching

Doughty, William L. John Wesley, Preacher. London: Epworth Pr., 1955.

Heitzenrater, Richard P. "John Wesley's Early Sermons."
   Proc. Wesley Historical Society 37, 4 (February 1970)
   110-128.

Holland, Bernard G. "A Species of Madness: The Effect of
   John Wesley's Early Preaching." Proc. Wesley Historical Society 39, 3 (October 1973), 77-85.

Lawson, John. Notes on Wesley's Forty-Four Sermons.
   London: Epworth Pr., 1946.

McCulloh, Gerald O. "The Discipline of Life in Early Meth-
   odism through Preaching and Other Means of Grace." In
   The Doctrine of the Church, pp. 161-181. Edited by Dow
   Kirkpatrick. New York: Abingdon, 1964.

Verhalen, Philip A. The Proclamation of the Word in the
   Writings of John Wesley. Rome: Pontificia Universitas
   Gregoriana, 1969.

         g.   Pastoral Care

Hill, Michael and Turner, Bryan. "John Wesley and the Ori-
   gin and Decline of Ascetic Devotion." In A Sociological
   Yearbook of Religion in Britain, vol. 4, pp. 102-120.
   Edited by Michael Hill. London: S. C. M., 1971.

Outler, Albert C. Evangelism in the Wesleyan Spirit. Nashville: Tidings, (1971).

_____. "Pastoral Care in the Wesleyan Spirit." Perkins
Journal 25, 1 (Fall 1971), 4-11.

Tripp, David. The Renewal of the Covenant in the Methodist
Tradition. London: Epworth Pr., 1969.

Ward, W. R. "The Legacy of John Wesley: The Pastoral
Office in Britain and America." In Statesman, Scholars
and Merchants: Essays in 18th Century History Presented to Dame Lucy Sutherland, pp. 323-350. Edited
by Anne Whiteman and others. Oxford Univ. Pr., 1973.

h.   Social Concerns

Body, Alfred. John Wesley and Education. London: Epworth Pr., 1936.

Collier, F. W. John Wesley among the Scientists. New
York: Abingdon, 1928.

Edwards, Maldwyn. John Wesley and the Eighteenth Century:
A Study of His Social and Political Influence. London:
Allen and Unwin, 1933.

Holland, Lynwood. "John Wesley and the American Revolution." Journal of Church and State 5 (1963) 199-213.

Hynson, Leon D. "John Wesley and Political Reality."
Methodist History 12, 1 (October 1973) 37-42.

Kingdon, Robert M. "Laissez-faire or Government Control:
A Problem for John Wesley." Church History 26, 4
(December 1957) 342-354.

MacArthur, K. W. The Economic Ethics of John Wesley.
New York: Abingdon, 1936.

Madron, Thomas W. "John Wesley on Race: A Christian
View of Equality." Methodist History 2, 4 (July 1964)
24-34.

_____. "Some Economic Aspects of John Wesley's Thought
Revisited." Methodist History 4, 1 (October 1965) 33-
45.

Prince, John W. Wesley on Religious Education. New
York: Methodist Book Concern, 1926.

i. Readings and Publishing

Baker, Frank. "A Study of John Wesley's Readings." London Quarterly and Holborn Review 168 (1943) 140-145; 234-242.

_____. "Wesley's Printers and Booksellers." Proc. Wesley Historical Society 22 (1939) 61-65; 97-101; 131-140; 164-168.

Boshears, Onva K. "John Wesley, the Bookman: A Study of His Reading Interests in the Eighteenth Century." Ph. D. dissertation, University of Michigan, 1972.

Herbert, Thomas Walter. John Wesley as Editor and Author. Princeton Univ. Pr., 1940.

Lawton, George. John Wesley's English. London: Allen and Unwin, 1962.

Rousseau, G. S. "John Wesley's Primitive Physic (1747)." Harvard Library Bulletin 16, 3 (July 1968) 242-256.

Scroggs, Robin. "John Wesley as a Biblical Scholar." Journal of Bible and Religion 28 (October 1960) 415-422.

j. Ecumenical Trends

Cannon, William R. "The Theological Stance of Methodism in the Ecumenical Movement." Methodist History 6, 1 (October 1967) 3-13.

Conversations between the Church of England and the Methodist Church: A Report. London: Epworth Pr., 1963.

Currie, Robert. Methodism Divided: A Study in the Sociology of Ecumenicalism. London: Faber, 1968.

Hunter, Frederick. John Wesley and the Coming Comprehensive Church. London: Epworth Pr., 1968.

Kissack, Reginald. Church or No Church: The Development of the Concept of Church in British Methodism. London: Epworth Pr., 1964.

Nash, David Foot. Their Finest Hour: Methodists and Anglicans. London: Epworth Pr., 1964.

Newton, John A. "The Ecumenical Wesley." The Ecumenical Review 24, 2 (April 1972) 160-175.

Outler, Albert C. "How Can We Arrive at a Theological
and Practical Mutual Recognition of Ministries?: A
Methodist Reply." In Councilium, vol. 74, pp. 83-91.
Edited by Hans Küng and Walter Kasper. New York:
Herder, 1972.

Rack, Henry D. The Future of John Wesley's Methodism.
London: Lutterworth, 1965.

Rupp, E. Gordon and Sykes, Norman. "Special Situation of
The Methodist Church in Relation to the Church of England and the Circumstances of the Breach." In Conversations between The Church of England and the Methodist Church, pp. 9-17. Edited by G. K. A. Bell, et al.
London: S. P. C. K.; Epworth Pr., 1958.

Smith, Warren Thomas. "Attempts at Methodist and Moravian Union." Methodist History 8, 2 (January 1970), 36-
48.

Todd, John Murray. John Wesley and the Catholic Church.
London: Hodder and Stoughton, 1958.

III. EIGHTEENTH CENTURY BRITISH METHODISM

Andrews, Stuart. Methodism and Society. London: Longmans, 1970.

Armstrong, A. The Church of England, the Methodists and
Society, 1700-1850. London: University of London Pr.,
1973.

Baker, Frank. "Methodism and the '45 Rebellion." London
Quarterly and Holborn Review 172 (1947) 325-333.

Bertrand, Claude-Jean. Le Méthodisme. Paris: Libraire
Armand Colin, 1971.

Burkhard, Johann Gottlieb. Vollständige Geschichte der
Methodisten in England aus glaubwürdigen Quellen. 2 vols.

in 1.   Nuremberg: Verlag der Rauschen Buchhandlung, 1795.

Davies, Rupert.   Methodism.   London: Epworth Pr., 1963.

_____, and Rupp, E. Gordon, eds.   A History of the Methodist Church in Great Britain,   Vol. 1.   London: Epworth Pr., 1965.

Dimond, Sidney.   The Psychology of the Methodist Revival: An Empirical and Descriptive Study.   Oxford Univ. Pr., 1926.

Gill F. C.   The Romantic Movement and Methodism: A Study of English Romanticism and the Evangelical Revival. London: Epworth Pr., 1954.

Halévy, Elie.   The Birth of Methodism in England.   Trans. and with an introduction by Bernard Semmel.   Chicago: Univ. of Chicago Pr., 1971.

Hammond, J. L. and B.   The Town Labourer, 1760-1832. London: Longmans, 1918.

Kent, J. H. S.   "Methodism and Revolution."   Methodist History 12, 4 (July 1974) 136-144.

Lee, Umphrey.   The Historical Backgrounds of Early Methodist Enthusiasm.   New York: Columbia Univ. Pr., 1931.

Lyles, A. M.   Methodism Mocked: The Satiric Reaction to Methodism in the Eighteenth Century.   London: Epworth Pr., 1960.

Minutes of the Methodist Conferences, from ... 1744, Vol. 1 (1744-1798).   London: Mason, 1862.

Myles, William.   A Chronological History of the People Called Methodists.   4th ed.   London: Cordeaux, 1813.

North, Eric McCoy.   Early Methodist Philanthropy.   New York: Methodist Book Concern, 1914.

Ramage, I.   Battle for the Free Mind.   London: Allen and Unwin, 1967.

Rupp, E. Gordon.   "Methodism in Relation to Protestant Tra-

dition. " In Proceedings of the Eighth Ecumenical Methodist Conference, Oxford, 28th August - 7th September,
1951, pp. 93-106. London: Epworth Pr., 1952.

_____. "Some Reflections on the Origin and Development
of the English Methodist Tradition. " London Quarterly
and Holborn Review 178 (1953) 166-175.

Sergant, William W. Battle for the Mind: A Physiology of
Conversion and Brain-Washing. Rev. ed. London: Pan
Books, 1963.

Semmel, Bernard. The Methodist Revolution. New York:
Basic Books, 1973.

Shipley, David C. "The Ministry in Methodism in the Eighteenth Century. " In The Ministry in the Methodist Heritage, pp. 11-31. Edited by Gerald O. McCulloh. Nashville: Board of Education, The Methodist Church 1960.

Taylor, E. R. Methodism and Politics, 1791-1851. Cambridge Univ. Pr., 1935.

Walsh, John D. "Methodism and the Mob in the Eighteenth
Century. " In Popular Belief and Practice (Studies in
Church History, 8), pp. 213-227. Edited by G. J. Cum-
ming and D. Baker. Cambridge Univ. Pr., 1972.

_____. "Origins of the Evangelical Revival. " In Essays
in Modern English Church History: In Memory of Norman Sykes, pp. 132-162. Edited by G. V. Bennett and
J. D. Walsh. London: Black, 1966.

Ward W. R. Religion and Society in England, 1790-1850.
London: Batsford, 1972.

Warner, W. D. The Wesleyan Movement in the Industrial
Revolution. London: Longmans, 1930.

Wearmouth, Robert F. Methodism and the Common People
of the Eighteenth Century. London: Epworth Pr., 1945.

Wilson, D. D. Many Waters Cannot Quench: A Study of Suf-
ferings of Eighteenth Century Methodism and Their Significance for John Wesley and the First Methodists. London: Epworth Pr., 1969.

CONTRIBUTORS

FRANK BAKER

Professor of English Church History, Duke University.

MICHAEL HURLEY

Director, Irish School of Ecumenics, Dublin.

LAWRENCE D. McINTOSH

Principal Librarian, Torrens University, Adelaide, South Australia; formerly Associate Professor of Theology and Assistant Director of the Library, Drew University.

ALBERT C. OUTLER

Research Professor of Theology, Perkins School of Theology, Southern Methodist University.

KENNETH E. ROWE

Assistant Professor of Church History and Methodist Librarian, Drew University.

E. GORDON RUPP

Dixie Professor of Ecclesiastical History, University of Cambridge.

MARTIN SCHMIDT

Professor of Church History and History of Doctrine, University of Heidelberg.

160

INDEX